The Christian and Divorce

The Christian and Divorce

by

Wendy Green

MOWBRAY
LONDON & OXFORD

Copyright © Wendy Green, 1981

ISBN 0 264 66796 4

First published 1981
by A. R. Mowbray & Co. Ltd
Saint Thomas House, Becket Street
Oxford, OX1 1SJ

Photoset by Redwood Burn Ltd.,
Trowbridge, Wiltshire

Printed in Great Britain by Richard Clay (The Chaucer Press)
Ltd., Bungay, Suffolk

I would like to express my gratitude to all who have made this book possible. To those who have re-lived their own heartache in order that others should find comfort, and those who have advised, corrected, and shared their knowledge. Thank you . . . very much.

Too many people have contributed to this book to re-create each one, with their own particular set of problems. The characters are therefore composites of people who have had similar experiences.

Contents

Introduction

Six years ago I would have been shocked if someone had suggested I should write a book about divorce. Divorce was a matter of remote statistics, something that happened to other people, not my family, my friends. Even when a close acquaintance confided that she was divorced and obviously wanted to talk out all the conflicts still surging through her mind, I didn't want to know. As far as I was concerned divorce was 'unscriptural', and therefore it didn't exist!

However, over the last three years the number of marriage breakdowns amongst my circle of friends has forced me to face the fact that divorce not only exists but is increasing at an alarmingly rapid rate. In 1971 there were 74,000 divorces. In 1977 there were 129,000.

It is tempting to conclude that divorce is 'too easy' – until you meet the men, women and children who have been through a marriage breakdown. Then you begin to wonder how anyone survives the adjustments and reconstruction a broken relationship involves. How do people cope? What are the problem areas? How can friends, relatives and counsellors help? What kind of people are getting divorced? How would we react if it was our marriage that was falling apart?

These, and many other questions, have formed the basis of my interviews with divorced people, the children of divorce, marriage guidance counsellors, clergy and representatives of the legal and medical professions. Their answers, together with the information I have gleaned from leaflets, books, reports and statistics, have given me a new appreciation of the dilemma divorce presents.

I still see divorce as a tragedy. Nobody escapes from a broken relationship, or a broken home, without suffering. It is not the ideal. The scriptures say that God hates divorce (Mal. 2.16). Jesus pointed men back to marriage as a creation ordinance when they tried to discuss divorce. Nevertheless he conceded that Moses permitted divorce 'For the hardness of your heart', and nobody knew the fallibility of mankind better than Jesus. We all 'fall short of the glory of God' continually. If divorce is a sin so is greed, envy, racism, covetousness, our lack of care for the elderly, our lack of concern about the Third World. I know I am not perfect, and far be it from me to cast the first stone at someone whose marriage has failed, especially if I do not understand, or never had to endure the problems they have had to face.

In a situation where there is one divorce to every three marriages (1977 statistics, Office of Population Censuses and Surveys – OPCS) none of us can afford to think our marriage is immune, or look down our noses at those whose marriage was not. I would always hope to see reconciliation as a first priority and more effort, teaching, counselling and concern about marriage and the family, but we must acknowledge the seriousness of the pressures working against them, pressures which affect both Christian and non-Christian. We cannot escape the facts. Divorce can and does happen. It is likely to go on happening. It would be ridiculous to expect otherwise in a society which has rejected God's standards and tried to explain away God. But divorce is not a pleasant experience. There are a lot of hurt, bewildered people in need of love and support. We may not condone divorce, but we can care; once we appreciate the conflicts, tensions and emotional and practical difficulties divorce creates.

I do not pretend to have found the answers to the problem of divorce. I am not a theologian. I am not a counsellor. I am not divorced. When I am confronted by someone else's agony I still feel inadequate, but at least I will now sit and listen, and leave the judgements to him who 'will judge ... with justice' (Acts 17.31 GNB).

My hope is that the experiences people have shared will be some consolation to others going through the misery of a marriage break-up, and some preparation for those who wittingly, or unwittingly, become the 'listening ear'.

One of the people I talked to asked the fellowship group to which she belonged at her Church if they could have a discussion on divorce one evening but her suggestion was not taken up. But such a discussion must surely have helped towards understanding the special problems of people, either within the Church fellowship or outside it, facing marriage difficulties or divorce.

If you think Christian marriages are immune you are mistaken. At a recent Christian conference, nearly ten per cent of the participants were experiencing, or had been through, a marriage break-up.

At the end of each chapter in this book, therefore, I have added a list of questions which could be used as a basis for discussion in Church fellowship groups, or alternatively for meditation in personal use.

1

Five people who faced divorce

Mrs Dee was the first person to bring divorce into my consciousness as something that actually happened to people I knew. She had been married for twenty years and divorced for ten, but a sense of guilt still nagged at the back of her mind. Had she been right to divorce her husband? Should she have stuck to him regardless of the effect the constant conflict was having on her and the children? She had made vows in church, before God, and came from a generation where your 'Yea was yea, and your nay meant nay'. She felt she had failed both herself and God. As she poured out her story I found I was asking myself, 'What would I have done in her situation?' It is a question I have been forced to answer again and again over recent months as people have shared the experiences that led to their marriage breaking up.

It is the easiest thing on earth to judge, or pre-judge; to set standards for others that, given their set of circumstances, we could well find impossible to maintain ourselves. Learning to live at the intimate level demanded by marriage is not easy, even in the most favourable conditions. How do people manage when the pre-wedding romance turns into a nightmare relationship, or when an apparently happy and satisfactory marriage is suddenly plunged into a frightening and unexpected divorce?

Marrying him was the biggest mistake
Mrs Dee had started out with high hopes. It was only after the wedding that the true nature of her partner began to reveal itself. He drank too much. There were

1

problems with money – their own and other people's. That led to trouble with the police, and glaring headlines across the local newspaper. He was in and out of work, had relationships with other women, and became violent very easily. Mrs Dee suggested a psychiatrist. Her husband retaliated by saying she should see one herself.

'He said I'd always seen him through rose-coloured spectacles,' she sighed. 'You couldn't get through to him. You should be able to talk to your husband without having a row. It was the biggest mistake of my life ever marrying him, but I was afraid of being left on the shelf. I tried to give him up when we were courting but he used to follow me. Wherever I was, he was. He could be very charming, till the drink got him. I went to the solicitor and talked about divorce twenty-five years ago but he didn't think I had enough grounds. In those days you didn't so easily get a divorce for mental cruelty, and at that time I hadn't had any physical cruelty. I would have divorced him sooner if I hadn't had any children, but I don't think I could have managed when they were little. As they got older I could see it affecting them. I felt they wouldn't stick it for much longer. It was either them, or him.' Mrs Dee felt obliged to divorce her husband after years of suffering and heart-searching.

Trust in a marriage
Barbara, a fresh-faced suburban housewife in her thirties, was plunged into divorce proceedings with very little forewarning. She had been married for thirteen years when she found out that her husband was going around with a much younger woman.

'Up till then,' she said, 'everything was fine. People thought we were a perfect pair. We had everything we needed, a lovely house, a car, two good kids. I thought it couldn't happen to me.' Then the blow fell. She sensed something was bothering her husband. He seemed to be growing away from the family. One Saturday lunchtime, hoping to joke him back into normality,

2

she asked if he had another woman. He replied that he had.

'It was the worst thing that ever happened to me in my life,' she said. 'We talked and talked and I gave him the choice of her or me. We moved house and he started a new job. The people I confided in told me it would happen again, but I couldn't go through life thinking I hadn't given him a chance. But the trust had gone, and trust in a marriage is something you don't think about until you haven't got it. Two years later he had gone again, only this time it was for good.'

An abandoned husband

A lot is written about abandoned wives, but not quite so much about abandoned husbands. Jeff realised there were tensions in his marriage within the first two or three years, but regarded them as problems of the early stages in marriage. His wife had a background of a broken home, and he realised that this might make things more difficult for her. Then, after the birth of their second child, she suffered badly with post-natal depression and was in and out of hospital. At the time his engineering job involved shift work, which didn't help the situation.

'It was murder,' he explained. 'We had violent rows, which I couldn't stand. I'd had an unhappy childhood too, and it brought back too many painful memories. We separated once but she had a nervous breakdown and I felt terribly guilty. I thought I had caused it, but I found out later she was having an extra-marital affair. We got back together for a year, but that was a terrible time. I was doing a lot of drinking, and she tried to commit suicide twice. After the second attempt she went back home to her mother in America. Then the trouble really began. She filed for divorce and petitioned for custody of the children. I contested it. She won everything, including the court costs. I was even supposed to pay her lawyer. I didn't do any of this. I pressed the matter through the English court and the children were made wards of court. But absolutely the

3

worst thing that could happen in this case happened. She snatched the children out of the country and now it's all going through the American courts again, and costing me a small fortune in legal fees.'

The ideal couple?

This may sound an extreme case. Andrew, a Church of England vicar, counselled many such couples in the front room of his vicarage home. The couples regarded him and his wife and three children as the epitome of family happiness. But when the front door closed behind them it was a different story.

'I've been married fifteen years,' he said, 'and although we've only been separated physically for eighteen months, we've been emotionally separated for about fourteen years. We tried to maintain a facade, especially after I was ordained, because then it's like living in a goldfish bowl. Everybody is looking at you. A Christian isn't supposed to have marriage difficulties, and a clergyman – God forbid! In the end I could stand the situation no longer. I could not continue a hypocritical existence where from the pulpit I had to say things to my congregation which were not true in my own life. And I think we both felt, for the sake of the children, it was better to be apart. So I walked out on my wife, which made her husband-less and homeless, and left me without a job.'

Pre-wedding problems

Mike's experience was no less painful, but decidedly shorter. His marriage lasted just nine months. There had been problems before the wedding day, but when he tried to break off the engagement his girl friend was so upset he decided to let things remain as they were, consoling himself with the false hope that things would be different when they were married. Even when friends advised they were too young to get married and pointed out the practical problems of starting new jobs, and a new life together, Mike shrugged off their fears. The marriage went ahead as planned.

'At first I couldn't see anything wrong,' Mike explained, 'apart from the fact that we used to argue a lot. But I thought that was fairly normal. We're both forthright and want our own way. I think we believed we could change one another. Now I realise people don't just change overnight, instead you tend to get more entrenched in your attitudes. You almost literally draw the lines of battle. Money was a big problem, and sex – that caused an incredible amount of friction, and made a lot of trivial problems seem much greater. We talked endlessly. We could see what the problems were, but we couldn't see ways in which either of us were prepared to change. There were so many things which led to differences it seemed rather silly having bothered to get married in the first place.'

Five people of different ages, different backgrounds, caught in a common predicament. All of them had entered into marriage with the usual hopes and expectations for a happy future but somewhere something had gone wrong. Divorce was no longer a statistic they read about in the papers. It was a frightening reality. How did they react? What would we do if it was our partner who said after a particularly unpleasant row, 'I'm going tomorrow and I'm not coming back?'

The reactions of these five people are included throughout the following chapters, together with those of others who had either been through divorce or who were in some way connected with helping divorcees.

Questions for discussion or personal meditation

1 How did you react to the experiences of the five people in this chapter?

　a) Did you make any attempt to enter into the person's experience?

　b) Did you make allowances for their character, background, youth, and the pressures of society (i.e. poor housing, limited finance, false expectations, permissiveness)?

c) Did you wonder if the stories would read differently if presented by the other partners?

d) Did you keep your mind open, or judge the situation according to *your* standards and circumstances?

e) Did you look inside yourself for inadequacies in your own character and relationships, and identify with the person at certain points?

2. Have you ever been asked for advice by someone with a marriage problem? How did you react?

3 Have you asked yourself if your marriage could be under threat? Would you acknowledge any responsibility for the areas that are less than perfect? Is there anything you could do to improve your relationship?

4 How might you react if it was your partner who said, 'I'm going tomorrow and I'm not coming back.'?

2

Emotions

It might be supposed that the practical problems connected with housing, children and finance would be the overwhelming consideration when a marriage breaks up. According to the people I interviewed this is not so. Coping with the emotions is the major difficulty, particularly in the early stages.

Shock
Where there had been little or no warning the intitial reaction was one of shock, or numbness. Barbara remembered breaking down and putting her hands over her eyes, as though it was the most horrible nightmare, when her husband first told her he wanted to marry another woman. Second time round she tried to 'be brave for the sake of the children' but after three days she collapsed in a mound of washing and howled her eyes out.

The depth of the shock seems to depend on the length and quality of the relationship and how aware people are that the marriage could be in danger.

Relief
Those whose relationship had deteriorated drastically were more likely to speak of relief or release. If they had experienced physical violence, or acute mental stress, people tended to turn to alcohol or drugs, or to bury themselves in their work in a desperate attempt to deaden their problems. Tension headaches and upset stomachs were commonplace. One man described physical symptoms of feeling more and more tired and

anxious as he got nearer to his home after work; the result of 'a combination of guilt and anxiety, a consciousness of failure and an inability to reach a solution.' When something happened to break such a deadlock, people were understandably relieved that they no longer had to live with 'that terrible unhappiness when you wake up in the morning and know you've got to face another day '

Anger

An instinctive reaction when something goes wrong is to blame someone else, and friends, family, clergy, doctors and God may all find themselves prime targets for the anger and resentment people feel towards their partner. Deserted women seem likely to react particularly violently, especially if another woman is involved. They spoke of 'hating their husbands' guts', of swearing to kill the husband or the 'other woman', and of wishing he could be 'plucked off the face of this earth'.

Sense of failure

Hatred of the partner comes second only to hatred of self. Nobody likes to admit to failure – whether it be an examination, a driving test, an interview, or a relationship. Yet we are conditioned from the cradle to regard marriage as the ultimate in human relationships. When the reality falls short of the ideal people can be torn apart by a sense of failure and guilt, which is often increased by the attitudes of those around.

Although the concept of guilt has been officially removed from divorce proceedings, the fact that divorces are heard in court is sufficient for the whole affair to carry overtones of criminal associations, and society still regards 'divorce' as a down-grading from the status of marriage. We speak of the 'failure' of a marriage. Divorced people often feel a failure as a person too. The length of the marriage, or the depth of the relationship makes little difference. Mrs Dee is still tortured by a sense of failure after twenty years of continuous effort. Mike went through a period of 'blackness', although his marriage lasted only a few months.

Often this sense of failure is linked to a low self-image. 'When someone leaves you there's an awful feeling of rejection,' Barbara explained, 'of not being good enough, of somebody else taking your place. You feel you're the lowest of the low.'

Sometimes this resulted in people believing they must be looking different, as though they had flashing lights, or horns on the forehead. So acute was this sense of embarrassment many people tried to avoid social contact, whether it was rushing up to their flat after work, or being afraid to fetch the washing off the line.

Lies, or half-truths, were often used as a way of avoiding awkward questions. One particular friend of ours managed to conceal the fact that she and her husband had parted for more than six months. 'I was worried that I would lose respect,' she admitted later. 'Then as the months went on I could lessen the blow by saying we had parted some time ago. I knew my friends wouldn't think any the worse of me, but I felt that a lot of older people would look down on me.'

Because they feel such failures, divorced people often expect others to have a low opinion of them too. In fact only one person seemed unconcerned what other people would think, and he was too immersed in his own predicament to notice. The more usual response was to joke aside awkward questions, or to build a protective veneer to hide their pain from the world.

Questioning
It might be possible to avoid answering the questions other people asked, but the questions that really hurt were the ones people were forced to ask themselves. 'I couldn't see why it had happened,' Mike declared. 'And I couldn't see how it would resolve itself. I was very confused about everything, my faith, my work, my identity as a person. I went round almost in a trance. Sometimes I was quite normal, other times I was quite bizarre in my behaviour.'

The sense of bewilderment was aggravated if the

spouse was torn between two partners, and could give no adequate explanation for abandoning the first. One wife was completely confused when her husband kept coming home and saying she had done nothing to cause the marriage to break up. On the contrary, he maintained she had always been a good wife to him. Why, then, had he found it necessary to go off with another woman, she asked herself.

In such circumstances it must be tempting to heap all the blame upon the partner's head, but most people do seem capable of examining themselves and the marriage for possible defects. Those who had been deserted in favour of another person asked two immediate questions. 'What's wrong with me' and 'What have I done?' Four years after her divorce Barbara is still asking herself and other people what went wrong. She frequently questions friends and neighbours about their married lives, and has come to the conclusion that she's not much different from anybody else. So why did her husband break up their home, and rush into a second marriage which seems very little different from his first?

Only Barbara, her husband and the 'other woman' could answer that question. But most people do try to identify why their marriage has failed, if only for their own peace of mind. The reasons are as varied as the people. Infidelity, immaturity, inability to change, false expectations, changing beliefs, mental illness, lack of forgiveness, lack of trust, lack of love, lack of communication, lack of commitment, lack of preparation, lack of perseverance. The list is endless.

Two important factors stand out prominently however. The number of young people who go ahead with a marriage in spite of serious doubts, and the number who allow themselves to drift apart, making little or no attempt to work at their deteriorating relationship.

Marriage guidance counsellors are rightly concerned about the number of couples who get trapped into the 'marriage machinery'. It must take a great deal of courage to call off the marriage preparations, especially as the big day looms nearer. But which is likely to be the bigger catastrophe – a broken engagement, or a broken marriage?

Mike has no doubt. He tried to break off his engagement, but abandoned the attempt when his girl friend became upset. Now, with the ruins of a marriage behind him, he wishes someone, somewhere, had been concerned enough to let him discuss all the doubts and uncertainties he was experiencing. 'I know at one point I felt that if it did go wrong we could always get a divorce,' he said. 'Looking back I realise what a ridiculous attitude that was. In the Prayer Book it says not to go into marriage unadvisedly or wantonly, and now I can see just how right that is.'

Unfortunately a number of people do go ahead with a marriage, despite serious doubts. There seems to be a common fallacy that once married everything will 'turn out right', and few people have a realistic picture of all that marriage entails.

So what happens when the economic, emotional and sexual expectations fail to materialise? Another unhappy set of divorce statistics, according to the OPCS monitor of divorces for 1977, shows that more than a quarter of divorces are for marriage which lasted five years or less. Older people may shrug their shoulders and tut about a generation that has always had things 'too easy' but nobody escapes from a broken relationship without a great deal of pain and suffering. Even those who had 'drifted apart' within a few months of the wedding ceremony did not emerge unscathed. Besides their own feelings of insecurity and self-doubt, many were left with the impression they had failed a major test of adult society. They might feign indifference, or callousness, but their bodies often denied this. Loss of weight, restlessness, irritability, lack of sleep were common symptoms. Bedtime was a particular battleground. The lucky ones might have friends who realised that evenings would be difficult, and took it in turns to occupy the time by chatting or playing records. But no matter how long they postponed the evil hour, sooner

11

or later they were forced to face the loneliness of an empty bedroom.

Depression

Eventually emotional and physical exhaustion took their toll. Initial reactions of shock and disbelief gave way to depression and despair as reality began to sink in. Sandra was only twenty when her husband abandoned her. At first she refused to believe that he had really gone. When she finally realised he was not coming back and she would be left with two young children, everything became an effort.

'You just put anything on,' she said. 'You don't bother with your hair. I didn't bother to eat. There seemed no point in anything, no reason. I got to the stage where I didn't want to get up in the morning. I used to hide under the bedclothes. I didn't want to face the day.'

Bereavement experience

Shock, anger, questioning, depression – symptoms more usually associated with bereavement. In fact doctors, psychologists and marriage counsellors all compare the loss of a partner by divorce to the loss of a partner by death. They speak of divorce as a bereavement experience, and refer to the divorcee as a bereaved person. There are the same psychological stages of grief to work through, and similar practical problems.

'I wish my husband had died,' said Barbara. 'I'm sure death must be easier to cope with than divorce.' An outrageous claim surely, one that could deeply incense someone recovering from the death of a partner? How can it possibly be justified?

For a start, the memories associated with divorce can be more painful. Barbara quoted a particular example of a picnic in a local park. The children pointed out a tree they had sat under the previous year – when their father was still with them. 'I would sit under any other tree but that tree,' said Barbara. 'Whereas if he'd died I would have wanted to go back there and re-live that time with him. At least I would have the comfort of knowing he still loved me.'

Another problem with bereavement by divorce is the lack of established rituals, associated with mourning. Most people accept that a bereaved person will need a lot of love and support, especially in the period between the death and the funeral. Not everyone is so understanding about the emotional upheaval experienced by a divorcee. Funerals may be harrowing but they are part of the ritual, the routine, evolved by society to help the mourners face the reality of death. In divorce there is no such ritual. Even appearance at court has become a thing of the past now that a large proportion of divorces are dealt with by special procedure. Only when the decree absolute arrives through the post are people forced to acknowledge that the marriage really has ended. And by that time the first novelty of knowing someone involved in a divorce may have worn off and friends fail to notice that a fresh bout of depression is imminent.

Items of clothing, personal belongings, photographs, places and a myriad other things may renew the sense of loss caused by a bereavement. The divorced have another problem to cope with – the body is still walking around. 'It's like living with a corpse,' Jeff said bitterly. 'It decays. It smells. It gets nasty.'

There are bound to be legal and financial problems connected with a death – wills, insurance, funeral expenses, death grants – but the legal and financial battles involved in divorce proceedings can continue indefinitely. Changes in material circumstances may require maintenance to be adjusted, decisions about the future of the children could mean protracted negotiations, one partner may re-marry and the property have to be divided. There can be disagreements about access, disagreements about discipline, jealousies, misunderstandings, further legal hassles.

Bereavement also involves a change of status. Widowhood carries with it a measure of respectability, and friends and neighbours are usually quick to rally round, particularly if there are children involved. With divorce the opposite can happen. Neighbours and former friends may actually avoid the divorced person, regarding them as a challenge, or a threat to their own marriage. Even in pure financial terms the divorced woman is in a worse position than the widow. Widows' pensions are higher than the allowance paid to a divorced woman, and most people have some form of insurance against death, although few, as yet, insure against divorce.

Whether the marriage is broken by death or divorce the bereaved are likely to have great difficulty in coming to terms with their loss, especially as the depth of the loss becomes increasingly apparent. Husbands or wives are not only sexual partners and companions, but breadwinners or homemakers, gardener, cook, handyman, and a parent for the children. So it is hardly surprising that the admission wards of our psychiatric hospitals are full of patients with problems associated with a broken relationship.

Suicide tendency

If the sense of loss or guilt become extreme, suicide may seem an attractive alternative. Over a quarter of the people I interviewed had either made suicidal gestures, or considered the possibility at some stage of divorce proceedings.

'There were times when I thought, "What's the point of existing?"' said Becky, a Catholic nurse whose marriage broke up after two years. 'I didn't seriously think of doing anything but it went through my mind, "If this is life, then I think I prefer death."' I wonder how we would react if one of our friends confessed they felt suicidal one sunny afternoon? Would we register shock, anger, rebuke or disbelief?

According to a doctor who makes it common practice to ask anyone who is extremely depressed or tense if they have ever considered suicide, it is better to face the possibility quite openly than shut one's eyes and pretend it could never happen. We may be hesitant for fear of putting ideas into their heads, but he believes it is more likely to release some of their tension if they can talk out their fears with someone who is prepared to listen and understand. If Sandra had had understanding friends during the first year of divorce she might not have been pushed to the extreme of taking an overdose.

'My life was in such a mess,' she said. 'My mind was in a turmoil. I wasn't all right when he was with me, and I wasn't all right when he was gone. So many people think you're OK, but you're not. I just wanted to go to sleep.'

One measure of the desperation people experience is the number of telephone calls received by Samaritans. In 1978, twenty-five per cent of the calls taken at our local branch were connected with marital or extramarital difficulties.

But suicide attempts, or threats, can be used as blackmail, against the partner, or the person befriending. How is it possible to distinguish between a cry for help and a genuine potential suicide? Do you call their bluff, or contact a professional?

The doctor advised that anyone who is intensely depressed should be encouraged to see their GP, or priest, or psycho-analyst, and if it seems necessary the friend or relative should stay with them, making sure that all obvious means of temptation are removed. 'It's much better to be safe than sorry,' he concluded, 'but experience will guide. If the person is a friend of yours you will know how seriously to take the things they say.'

But even the most experienced counsellors cannot always tell how desperate a person really is. Aren't they afraid they could make a mistake that could prove tragic? 'If someone wants to commit suicide you can't really stop them,' said one counsellor. 'You've got to give the person responsibility for themselves. You can only help them to look at the consequences of their actions.'

15

Need for tranquillisers

Another disturbing factor is the number of people receiving medication. Every woman I spoke to had taken tranquillisers or anti-depressants at some stage during or after divorce proceedings. A much smaller proportion of men had been prescribed drugs, but a number suffered stomach upsets, or turned to drink, sex, heavier smoking, or pornographic films. I asked the marriage counsellor why so many people appeared to need tablets. 'That just shows how traumatic divorce is,' he replied. 'People who are bereaved usually need sleeping tablets but a wise doctor weans them off pretty quickly. They're probably hesitant to prescribe them in the first place.' But are they? And do they explain to their patients what they are prescribing?

'I was in such a state of shock that my mother sent me to the doctor,' said Barbara. 'And instead of listening and helping he gave me valium. That seems to be the answer to everything. Take these three times a day, and come back if you don't feel better. But they just put me in a state of daze. I walked around like a zombie, doing everything Mum told me. I couldn't think straight. I remember buying a load of cat food, and we've got a dog.'

Maybe that was the shock, the numbness? Not necessarily. 'Feeling like a zombie' can be a characteristic side-effect of some anti-depressants and tranquillisers. But how many people are told that, and do they really want a handful of pills when they go to the surgery in any case?

A doctor practising in an urban area with more than the average proportion of marriage breakdowns believes that giving medication may appear the quickest and easiest way out. But what people really want is something much more demanding – time to discuss their problems. Time is a precious commodity though, especially when there is a waiting room full of other patients. Sometimes he finds it is only possible to have a brief discussion to relieve the immediate tension, then arranges for longer appointment at a later date. He may

16

prescribe tablets as an aid through the difficult early stages, but only as an addition, or supplement, to discussion.

'I try to make it plain that *no* tablet will take the problem away,' he said. 'They are only a bonus on top of what the individual can do to help themselves cope with their problems. But this needs explaining repeatedly.'

Indeed it does – and by a greater number of doctors, for the long-term effects of some drugs can be just as frightening as the unexpected side-effects. 'I didn't realise just how heavy these things are,' said Barbara. 'It was very hard to get off them afterwards. I did try, but I couldn't focus properly. I panicked as I went to go into a big department store. When I went to see the doctor he was horrified that I'd stopped taking the tablets. I was suffering withdrawal symptoms. But he never told me any of this when he prescribed them. It took me four months to get off the things.'

Maybe Barbara was unfortunate in her choice of doctor? Then so were a number of other women. The majority were glad of tablets as a temporary measure but they were extremely grateful that with the support of their family and their own inner resources they had not found it necessary to continue taking them for any length of time. But few had received any indication as to what the tablets were, or what they could, or could not, do. So, how essential are they? Is it important to take them if they are prescribed? What about people whose religious beliefs might make them hesitant about taking drugs?

'I see no reason why Christians should object to using the normal medical means of help (that is, drugs),' said a Christian doctor. 'One has to have a right perspective. Nobody wants to become over dependent on drugs, but at the same time they are a very real practical help in many medical conditions, such as stress and depression.'

Questions for discussion or personal meditation

1. Think back to a time when you experienced a sense of failure or shock such as the death of a close relative, a broken engagement, failing an examination or a driving test, redundancy or unemployment.
   a) How did you react?
   b) What emotions did you experience?
   c) How did it affect you physically?
   d) What did you feel like when you had to tell other people?
   e) *Could* you tell other people?
   d) What defence mechanisms do you use to hide your feelings of failure or inadequacy?
2. None of us like to admit we have made a mistake so how can we help people see that their own actions and attitudes may have contributed to the failure of their marriage?
3. Do you agree that divorce is a bereavement experience?
   a) What reactions might you expect from someone going through a divorce?
   b) Could you cope with them?
   c) Would you be strong enough to take their anger and resentment?
4. What symptoms might lead you to believe someone was suffering from depression? What would you do?
   a) Should you expect them to 'snap out of it'? (Say why, or why not.)
   b) Would you advise them to see their doctor? (Say why, or why not.)
What factors are likely to prolong depression in divorce proceedings?
5. Are tablets a blessing, a curse, or a 'bonus on top of what the individual can do to help themselves cope with their problems?'
6. How would you cope if one of your friends . . .
a) said they felt suicidal?
b) made a suicide attempt?

3

Meeting immediate needs

If talk can be as valuable as tablets, but doctors don't always have the time to talk, are they able to refer patients on for further help? Some large group practices will have counsellors working on their premises, and occasionally a doctor may refer a patient on to Marriage Guidance or a local clergyman. Whether they go is a different matter.

But the majority of people turn to friends or relatives for help and support. This is a frightening thought when the problems are so deep, and the consequences so far-reaching. How can ordinary laymen cope, with little or no training? They can listen for a start – without showing embarrassment or condemnation, however shocking they may find the disclosures.

'People think you don't want to talk,' explained Jeff. 'But it's like when someone dies. It's the natural and obvious thing to do. There's no need to change the subject if divorce comes into the conversation, as long as people don't press you to answer questions you're not ready to face '

Don't pressurise. Don't judge. Don't condemn. It all sounds so negative. What if somebody obviously needs to talk, but doesn't know where to begin? 'Be patient,' advised a doctor. 'Sit in silence till they're ready to speak, perhaps quietly praying for them while they're going through the difficult stage of making up their-minds what they want to say.'

Need of time
But we are more used to rush and bustle – instant com-

munication, instant foods, instant satisfaction of our every want. Isn't there a quicker solution, an easier answer than sitting and listening? Apparently not. Divorce, like bereavement, is such a shock to the system, the bereaved person not only needs time to talk, but time to recover, and untold damage can be done by well-meaning friends whose stock of sympathy runs so short they expect the sufferer to 'snap out of it' in a matter of weeks.

The need will be most acute in the early stages, particularly if there was little to indicate that a marriage breakdown was imminent. Shock, a sense of failure and guilt are not easy emotions to live with, especially when they are coupled with all kinds of practical fears for the future. Decisions cannot be made overnight, nor depression dealt with at one blow. Friends and relations who apply undue pressure, or encourage a divorcee to take a one-sided view could well be increasing the amount of time a person takes to adjust to their new situation.

Need of compassion

A more constructive attitude could be to imagine yourself in place of that person, experiencing a distressing range of emotions. At such a time silence is more healing than artificial words, and sympathetic understanding a greater balm than pity. Compassion may be an old-fashioned word, but when an individual is bruised and battered by the pain of divorce the fact that someone is able to enter into their sorrow and share it with them can be a vital link in the process of healing. When Sandra's friend wept with her as she was recounting the hurt of her marriage breakdown that meant more to her than any counselling session.

We have developed all kinds of subtle defence mechanisms, however, to prevent our friends from displaying any form of emotion that may upset our own equilibrium. If we find someone sobbing their heart out we are likely to phone for the doctor, or tell them sharply to pull themselves together. In reality it would help more if we allowed them to pour out their feelings. Accepting their anger, whether it is directed at us, their partner, or God, could be helping them towards an acceptance of themselves and the new situation. On the other hand, blame and condemnation could mean they will suppress their grief and possibly suffer prolonged emotional and physical ill health.

Because we are unused to expressing emotion, those who do 'let go' in the presence of a trusted friend may well be overwhelmed with fresh feelings of shame and guilt – and feel they need to apologise for their lack of control. Others tormented by thoughts of suicide, or emotions they would never have dreamt possible, assume they must be 'abnormal'. If friends can help them to understand such reactions are common to anyone passing through a bereavement experience they will be performing a very valuable service.

Need of reassurance
On the other hand, if divorcees get the impression they are being 'weighed in the balance and found wanting' they will only be confirmed in their belief that they are failures, fully deserving whatever wrath God or man may care to administer. Colin, a minister and marriage guidance counsellor, stressed the importance of not being judgemental. 'People in a broken marriage know they've failed,' he said. 'They don't need to be told. We have to remember we're all sinners in need of forgiveness. We need to be humble and recognise that our own marriage may not be immune. We're all susceptible to the wiles of the devil.'

Friends need to recognise their own vulnerability, particularly when they are counselling, or consoling, someone already overburdened by their own inadequacies and desperately needing the reassurance of God's forgiveness and love.

'It's important to help them realise we *all* have failings, and that Christ came into the world not for the righteous but for sinners,' a Christian doctor emphasised. 'He shares our sorrows and our failings with us to

21

the extent of the mental and spiritual suffering he endured on the cross. Even if we feel desperate and right at rock bottom he's been down to that level and can share it with us. If we have a Christian faith we still have hope even though everything in a practical sense seems to have gone wrong. There's *no* situation that is irredeemable. We're not alone in our suffering, however alone we may feel.'

Need to rebuild confidence

Because divorce can leave people with little self-esteem, an important part of helping them back to normality is helping to re-build their sense of worth. In the early stages they may need loving friends and relatives to assume control of the day-to-day running of their lives. But once the initial shock has worn off most people need to be allowed to gradually pick up the reins, and resume their normal tasks. If not, they may lose complete confidence in themselves and their ability to cope. They may also need encouragement in making, or maintaining, relationships if their confidence has been badly shattered by the divorce.

Many divorced people pass through a period of blackness and despair when they can see nothing but a bleak future ahead of them. Although friends should not pretend that the going will be anything but tough, they can also paint a more positive picture. Children, financial provision and a sympathetic and supportive family can be shown as valuable assets. People who have been through a similar experience and survived may help them to see that life can be worthwhile in spite of all that has happened, that there is a glimmer of light at the end of the tunnel. Birthdays and anniversaries, people and places, are bound to revive painful memories, but being prepared, and accepting that this is normal will help more than trying to avoid possible sources of distress.

Readjustment

Just how long a person may take to readjust depends on

a number of factors, although it has been estimated that recovery from a bereavement can take anything from two to five years. Temperament has a lot to do with how quickly a person recovers. An outgoing, well-balanced personality will more quickly realise that life can and must go on, than someone who is introspective and withdrawn. One person will have re-made some form of life for themselves and their children within a couple of years of divorce; another may still be experiencing psychological hang-ups ten years later.

'If I have an anaesthetic I come out of it crying and sobbing, heartbroken,' said Mrs Dee. 'When I had my last operation the sister said she'd never seen anyone so upset coming round. She knew I'd got emotional problems.'

An individual's ability to adjust will also depend on their past history and home background. Several people with unhappy childhoods spoke of marital conflict and breakdown reviving the old feelings of rejection and bitterness. The circumstances surrounding the divorce are also bound to make a difference. The partner who leaves home with a third person is likely to be a good deal happier than the one who is left behind. Disagreement over the children, accommodation and maintenance can all prolong the agony. Not surprisingly those left in impoverished circumstances with inadequate accommodation found greatest difficulty picking up the pieces.

Whether a partner is left in isolation, or has outside interests and friends will also affect the speed of recovery. Men might have work to divert their attention during the day, but the women are more likely to have the companionship of the children during the long, lonely evenings. Many women spoke of the incentive children had been when building a new life. 'You can't afford to have a breakdown when you've got children,' Barbara explained.

Need of help with children
But if divorce is a bereavement experience for an adult, what effect does it have upon the children? Parents,

23

clergy, marriage guidance counsellors, doctors and psychiatrists all agree that divorce can be more devastating than death for a child. Children find lack of finality particularly difficult to accept. To all intents and purposes one parent appears to have abandoned them, yet they return periodically, expecting everything to be just as before. Even if a child has been aware that there is disunity in the home, he may still be totally unprepared for the final split. Those who have no inkling that there is anything wrong find the shock even more traumatic. If no explanation is attempted the child's bewilderment is complete.

How far are parents capable of understanding their child's grief at a time when they are barely coping with their own sense of loss? It seems to depend mainly on the circumstances and the quality of the relationship between parent and child. Some parents openly acknowledged their inadequacy. Others surprised themselves by answering their children's questions with a frankness and lack of bias they would never have believed possible.

'It's a matter of helping the parents to look at the problem from the child's point of view as well as their own,' a doctor explained. 'In a divorce everybody suffers, and the more closely they are related the more likely they are to be hurt. The child who is bereaved of a father through divorce is going to suffer just as much as the wife who loses her husband. Everybody has needs, and everybody needs to help each other.'

If friends and relatives rally round and let the children share in their family life this can be one way of helping. Financial help in the form of pocket money, extras for outings and holidays, shared meals, shopping expeditions, and presents of clothing are also appreciated. When a mother is having problems with discipline the support of a male relative can be invaluable, as can the patient understanding of a granny or grandad. They probably have more time to sit and let the child unwind than a single parent trying to cope with a job, a home, a family, and their own emotions.

Need of love and support
Whatever the papers and popular opinion may say, divorce is not easy, and divorced people need a lot of care and a lot of love. Just to know that someone is there, getting on quietly with the day-to-day tasks will not compensate for the loss of the partner, but it can go a long way to alleviating some of the pressures.

'In the early stages they can't cope with everyday things,' explained Colin, the marriage counsellor. 'Basically they need the sort of loving care you'd expect from a brother or sister if they'd lost their partner by death.' Whether or not they get it is a different matter.

Questions for discussion or personal meditation

1. a) Are you a talker or a listener?
   b) Can you get beyond your own interests and concerns to consider someone else's need for help?
   c) Is listening sufficient? (Say why, or why not.)
2. What pitfalls should we beware of if someone comes to us for advice?
3. How can we listen and receive someone's feelings without being judgemental? Does that mean we must suspend all sense of right and wrong? How necessary is it to ask ourselves why someone behaves like they do, and allow them to face up to possible faults in themselves and their relationships in their own time and at their own pace?
4. What kind of needs will someone experiencing a marriage break-up have? Are we capable of expressing the 'kind of loving care you'd expect from a brother or sister'? (Say why, or why not.)
5. How can we help someone rebuild their confidence? What setbacks might we expect?
6. Why is divorce more devastating than death to a child? How might a child reveal his/her emotions? Should a parent be expected to cope with their child's hurt and bewilderment alone? (Say why, or why not.) What practical help and support might the family, fellowship or friends give?

4

The need to talk

'It was only with great difficulty I began to talk about my wife leaving. The first person I told was one of my colleagues at work. He sat down on the chair and didn't say a word for a while.'

'I spoke to friends about my problems. They were very sympathetic.'

'We did talk. That was one part of our relationship that was good. We could always discuss things although I felt he twisted the discussion round and didn't really consider my point of view.'

'I didn't have anyone to talk it over with. I just had to get on with it.'

'Sometimes we under-estimate the value of just pouring out our troubles to a listening ear, then getting on with the marriage again.'

'I don't think either of us could talk to the other. I think, in a sense, our independence just became selfishness in the end.'

'I talked about it to everyone. I wanted sympathy. I wanted to know somebody cared. Your life seems so very empty.'

'Talking to somebody is a great help. Once you've got over the initial difficulty of saying, "I've got a problem."'

We live in an age of communication – telephones, telegraphs, satellites relaying instant news from the other side of the world. So it is hardly surprising that talking formed such an important part of the healing and adjusting process. But who did people talk to? Could they find someone who would stop and listen in a world which seems dominated by television, timetables and time and motion studies?

Telling the families

One group who had to be consulted fairly early on were the parents and in-laws, no matter how reluctant a couple might be to reveal that the marriage was in difficulty. Many postponed the unpleasant moment as long as possible, dreading an adverse reaction and the upset they sensed the news would create. Mrs Dee sat outside the house in the car, so great was her sense of shame and fear, when her husband went in to talk to her mother about a particular crisis point in their marriage. Mike took over a week before he could bring himself to tell his parents his wife had left, and then it only came out between sobs in answer to a direct question.

Why is it that so much tension is generated when confiding in our 'nearest and dearest'? Often the answer seemed to be linked to the ideals and expectations of the parents. When Mrs Dee first began to mention the possibility of divorce, society was far less lenient in its attitudes and her parents were no exception. Coming from a fairly strict Wesleyan background, they found the whole idea of divorce abhorrent and soon began to apply pressure for the couple to stay together. Mike faced a similar problem, in the 70's. He had tried to discuss his pre-wedding doubts with his parents but they had dismissed them as cold feet. Surely they would feel some sense of moral responsibility for their son's predicament? On the contrary. His father was a lay reader in the local church and both parents were totally opposed to any suggestion of divorce, quoting scripture and church doctrine to support their case.

The families that seemed to be most understanding were the ones where there had already been some element of marital disruption in the family history. Parents might appear conservative in their attitudes, but could be surprisingly understanding if they had previously experienced the heartache involved in a brother's or sister's broken marriage. If it was the parents' own marriage that had foundered the child might dread hurting the parent a second time, especially if they had expressed fear that the children might make

27

a similar mistake. But once they plucked up courage and confided their problems the shared trouble could draw them closer together.

On the other hand, if there had already been an element of alienation or antagonism in the relationship divorce could drive an even deeper wedge between parent and child. Several feared telling their parent about their problems because they knew the response would be, 'I told you so.' Where the parent took sides, especially against their own offspring, feelings were particularly bitter. 'My father always had a soft spot for my wife,' Jeff declared angrily. 'He swore blind it was my fault we split up. He didn't know what had been going on and the things she had done to me.'

Families also complicated matters by refusing to assist if the couple were struggling to maintain a fairly civilised relationship despite the divorce. One woman was particularly distressed because her family refused to have any contact with her husband, whom they saw as the villain of the piece. She felt it was important to retain some sense of normality for the sake of the child, but if 'he' was visiting they would stay outside rather than enter the house.

It is argued that families can speed up the deterioration of a relationship by interfering too much, but social services seem a very inadequate substitute for the love and support of a caring family. When a marriage has disintegrated and one parent is struggling to cope alone, families can play a vital part in helping them survive. Young people may present a tough exterior, and insist they 'can manage', while in reality they are really hurt and bewildered if their parents fail to understand, or be concerned about their dilemma. Once the marriage had broken up the majority did receive practical support in terms of babysitting, household repairs, decorating, offers of accommodation and financial assistance, but few received any advice or guidance when the marriage may have been salvaged.

Much criticism has been levelled at the Asian system of arranged marriages, but there the whole family is involved at all levels; arranging, celebrating and maintaining. This is not without its own abuses but at least an inexperienced couple are not left to sink or swim completely unaided. Then if the marriage does stand in danger of breaking up the problems can be shared between the families and their advisors. Western society may appear to be working towards a more democratic individualised system where people are less dependent on their parents, but how far individuals are capable of surviving as isolated units is debatable.

Talking to the in-laws
In-laws are also capable of increasing or alleviating the distress of a marriage breakdown. Reactions varied from the couple whose main concern appeared to be that the wedding presents from their side of the family should remain in their daughter's possession, to the family who were upset that the marriage had broken up and tried to maintain friendly contact with both parties. The most hurtful reactions were from those who broke off all forms of communication when the relationship had previously appeared to be quite friendly.

Barbara had been very fond of her parents-in-law and just couldn't understand why they wanted nothing more to do with her. 'Maybe they were ashamed, or maybe it was easier to do that than to be split in two. After all, blood is thicker than water, and they only heard one side of the story.' Whatever the reason behind their actions that hurt remains in Barbara's life, and has to be faced again and again when the children visit their grandparents, or when letters and cards contain no word of greeting for the former daughter-in-law.

Family funerals can also be a cause for more than the normal share of grief. One woman whose former father-in-law died had every intention of attending the funeral, until she realised her ex-husband had re-married and she was no longer part of the family. 'I was very fond of dad,' she mourned. 'Yet I felt an outsider and didn't think it was right to go.'

Talking to friends and neighbours
If the family didn't want to be involved, who did people turn to for support? 'The first person I told was my next-door neighbour,' said one woman. 'My family were away at the time so I had no one to turn to but a few close friends. I could either pick up the phone, or call in on them. I had to talk it out. That's the time you realise who your friends really are.'

Many people reiterated this statement speaking of real friends, close friends, good friends, one good friend. People who had been through a similar situation were particularly helpful. They understood the problems, and could offer some hope and reassurance if they had managed to come out the other side of the experience still sane.

Decidedly unhelpful were the so-called friends who wanted to know all the details, gave instant and conflicting advice gleaned from magazines, then lost interest once the divorce had gone through.

Those who came down in judgement were equally off-putting. Mike, already contending with pressure from his parents, found his problem doubled by friends who insisted he should continue with the marriage. Mrs Dee had a neighbour who frequently reminded her that Mr Dee was her partner 'for better or for worse.' Arguments proved useless. In the end Mrs Dee lost her patience and told the neighbour she might think differently if she had to live with him. 'Once he went out and swore at her,' she said, 'and she was going to get a solicitor's letter – just for that one incident. I put up with that. It was a minor thing compared to the rest.'

The sympathetic ear
There seems to be a world of difference between genuine friendship willing to share the hurt, and the casual, off-hand inquiries of acquaintances and colleagues. Mike was one of several people who found it very difficult to talk at all about his marriage break-up. 'I didn't feel ashamed,' he said, 'but I felt exposed. I knew that to talk about it would bring it all to the front

of my mind, and I didn't want to do that.'

It may not be easy to express our hidden feelings honestly and openly, but trying to pretend they do not exist will fool only the most callous and indifferent, and can create psychological and emotional barriers later. One woman who visited Marriage Guidance had bottled up her emotions for nineteen years. After an hour's conversation she felt she could cope again . . . and did not need to make a second appointment. But what a pity she had waited nineteen years before she felt able to let go of her burden.

What did people expect, or hope for, when they found a listening ear and poured out all their troubles? Understanding and sympathy seemed to be the basic requirements. One person explained, 'You can't go into an empty room and say out loud to yourself, "My problem is such and such." Someone with a sympathetic ear does seem to help.'

It sounds simple, but it's not always so easy for the person who finds themself in the role of the listening ear, feeling helplessly and hopelessly inadequate. What can they do? Alison, a marriage guidance counsellor, advised just letting people talk and talk and talk. 'It's amazing how few people have anyone they can really talk to,' she said. 'All you need to do is listen, then offer them love and acceptance of themselves, and the conviction that time will heal.'

She did offer several words of warning however. Don't take sides; rather help them to understand there are two views of every marriage. Don't start giving advice; even trained counsellors are told not to give advice unless it's purely practical. Don't get out of your depth; refer people on to a doctor or a trained counsellor or a social worker if the problems start getting out of hand. And above all remember that all this will involve time, and maybe a good deal of heart-searching on your own part, especially if you find yourself getting depressed because you can't cure a crumbling marriage with a wave of a magic wand or an instant prayer.

Sometimes there are practical things friends and

family can do to help if the couple are still together. Looking after the children may relieve some of the pressure and give the couple time to actually *listen* to one another. All too often one partner says, 'You're out every night of the week,' and the other disputes it, when what they're really trying to tell the partner is that it *feels* as if they are out every night. Time and money may be limited, but a weekend or an evening alone together could be a sound investment, and certainly cheaper than a divorce.

Questions for discussion or personal meditation

1. Are you able to discuss problem areas in your life?
   a) Would you be able to ask for help if your marriage was in danger? (Say why, or why not.)
   b) Who would you most dread telling? Why?
   c) How do you think you might feel in relationship to God?
   d) How do you think you might feel in your relationship to other Christians?
2. How would you react if your son or daughter, or a close friend, plucked up courage to tell you they were considering a divorce?
   a) Would you be shocked, horrified, distressed, angry, or disbelieving?
   b) How would you deal with your reactions, in view of the effect they can have on someone already conscious of failure and rejection?
3. Could you help someone see beyond their immediate pain and anger in a marriage breakdown? How? How would you try to prevent yourself judging, or taking sides?
4 When confronted by someone else's suffering . . .
   a) Is it necessarily a bad thing to feel inadequate? Why?
   b) How can we safeguard against the temptation to 'pass the buck'?
   c) What considerations need to be taken into account if we become involved?
   d) What should we do if we get out of our depth?

5
Counselling

Re-exploring a relationship may be painful but how much greater the pain if husband suddenly turns round and says, 'Right, that's it,' as Sandra's did. She didn't have a chance to talk to her husband. Others realised they were drifting apart but couldn't communicate across the rift.

Jeff knew there was something seriously wrong with the relationship between his wife and himself and tried to get her talking about it. But she had never been a great talker, preferring to bottle up her problems until she made a sudden and apparently irrational decision. He thought she didn't share enough. She thought he was too glib, because he tried to work out his problems by talking them through. One of the basic skills of marriage counselling is trying to bridge this communication gap, to help people share with each other the things they have avoided.

Talking to the partner
Does that mean couples have the ability to solve their problems simply by talking about them? Some can, others need outside help, but the younger the couple and the marriage the more they seem to be at risk. The under twenty-fives I interviewed all spoke of not being willing to change, or of the other person refusing to change, and the divorces for that age-group have trebled since 1970 according to OPCS statistics (winter 1979).

'Several times we sat down and had a talk,' said Sam, a building site worker, who stayed with his wife for just over a year, 'but being me and knowing myself, it was like water off a duck's back. I've never listened to anybody really. I could see what she meant, but we had different interests. We just wound up going our own ways.'

I asked Colin why so many people went into marriage with the idea that they could change their partner. 'That shows a basic disrespect for the other person,' he replied. 'You've got to ask why they married them in the first place. What attracted them to that person without the changes they were hoping for? I think people expect happiness and compatibility to come fairly easily and quickly, and it's a tremendous shock when it doesn't. People's expectations are unrealistic in all kinds of ways – economically and sexually. They're fed enormously by the media, women's magazines, TV, romantic novels, advertisements. Then if the expectations are blasted very early on some people don't get over the shock. To build a good marriage you need a lot of resources. You've got to have strength, courage, faith and persistence, and if we're producing a generation of children who've had these things eroded then it's going to reproduce.'

He sees one glimmer of hope in pre-marriage counselling, not just at the level of engaged couples, but at an even younger age, in schools. Talking to students and creating the idea that it's not a failure to go and ask for help will, hopefully, build a generation who will be less hesitant to go for counselling.

Over the past few years sex education has been an important part of most primary and secondary schools' curriculum. The 1978 Lichfield Report, *Marriage and the Church's Task*, suggests that personal relationships should be a normal part of the curriculum too. Teachers may complain of the pressure of exams and the number and range of subjects they are required to teach, but if a generation of children are growing up lacking a model on which to build their relationships, surely we are laying up problems for the next generation, unless something is done now?

34

The report also stresses the importance of marriage preparation, but acknowledges that many parishes are so large the minister cannot possibly cope alone. In some areas the burden is now shared between clergy. In others, inter-church counselling for engaged couples is provided, and solicitors, doctors and bank managers are invited to share in the sessions. Secular agencies such as Marriage Guidance report a slow but steady rise in the number of engaged couples requesting interviews, but like most counselling services find there are never enough counsellors for the number of people requiring help.

Even if there were sufficient counsellors, pre-marriage counselling can be too late. Young couples in the full flush of romantic love are unwilling, or unable, to face up realistically to possible difficulties once the honeymoon is over. A Catholic priest, working in an urban area, saw lots of the problems in marriage going back to the parents and their relationships, and felt the real need was to educate the parents. The phrase 'visiting the iniquity of the fathers upon the children' had taken on a new significance for him since he had seen the havoc that could be wrought by a broken home.

He was not alone in his anxiety. Many divorced people were themselves worried about the effect their broken relationship could have upon the children. Jeff's wife was the product of a broken home and he could see history repeating itself before his eyes. 'But how do you break the chain?' he grieved.

Maybe Jeff, and others worried about the effect a broken relationship can have, are already half way to coping with the situation. 'At least they're aware of the dangers,' said Alison, the marriage guidance counsellor. 'The problems come when someone denies there can be any damage.'

Hopefully, awareness doesn't just mean anticipating trouble and worrying yourself silly but using that knowledge constructively when problems do arise. Similarly, children of divorce need not decide that their own marriage must be heading for disaster. Providing they can face the effect divorce has had upon them and their relationships, it can give them a determination that they will not make the same disastrous mistakes.

Counselling one year into marriage could do a lot to avert potential crises, for it is then that couples are beginning to face up to areas of conflict. The difficulty is getting them to admit it.

If couples cannot be helped to communicate, there is a real danger that frustrations will build up to such a pitch they will erupt into mental or physical violence. Battered wives, and husbands, are a distressing facet of modern society. Although the breakdown of a marriage may be proved on five different grounds, over one third of the divorce decrees granted to women in 1977 were on grounds of 'cruelty'. It may be argued that we live in a violent age, or that there has always been violence inside marriage. It is only now that people are beginning to admit it openly. Whatever the cause, this is one area where people 'at risk' need to seek help at an early stage, however ashamed or frightened they may be.

Talking to the minister
Statistics underline the fact that divorce is increasing annually. OPCS figures show that in 1974 there were 113,500 divorces, in 1975 the figure had risen to 120,522, in 1976 to 126,694 and in 1977 to 129,053.

Given the size and scope of marriage problems, and these annual increases in divorce, the easiest course of action would appear to be to close the eyes to the situation, or give up in despair. Colin had trained as a teacher and a priest but felt completely at a loss to deal with the number of marital and family breakdowns he was surrounded by in a parish situation. He felt he needed further training before he could even begin to understand the problems. His concern propelled him into Marriage Guidance. Soon Alison, his wife, was undertaking similar training. 'It's no good saying, "These are the scriptures. This is what it says," when a couple are battering each other, and moving out to Mum's,' she explained.

The 1978 Lichfield Report, already referred to, suggests that clergy training should include courses in counselling in marriage and family life. But even if the suggestions are implemented, will those courses be given a large enough slice of the college curriculum and professional staffing? Colin believes the problem is so central to society, and to the parishes in which clergy will be working, that nothing but the best will suffice.

'The Church should be communities that shine like beacons as having stable relationships, that have got their priorities right,' he said, 'men and women who don't work all God's hours to get extra money but who believe their family life is more important, even if it means taking a lower standard of living. We should be sharing our joys, our failures in marriage, and allowing our sexuality to be more seen, more open. Once the vicar has demonstrated that it is safe to review your inadequacies and doubts and inhibitions, then the relationships in the rest of the fellowship will open up and others become involved in the sharing and healing processes.'

It is not an easy option however. The clergy are already working under stress in many areas, and do not always have the time or the skill to undertake pastoral care at this depth. Several ministers spoke of the 'floodgates opening' once it became known that the vicar was capable of helping with marriage problems. So it would seem that clergy should not be expected to bear the burden alone, but be encouraged to share the load with other clergy, counselling agencies and concerned lay people.

But are the clergy always willing and able to help? The Church is responsible for solemnizing nearly fifty per cent of all marriages, according to OPCS statistics, marriage 1977. How much responsibility do they assume when that same marriage is breaking apart?

One minister told Mrs Dee to leave her husband, another said everything to try and bring them together. They were quick to dole out advice, but what about practical care and concern? Mrs Dee laughed. 'They never came to see how I was getting on or anything,' she said. 'I told one that my husband had gone and he just said, "Well, go on down to Social Security and get yourself some money."' Perhaps Mrs Dee had an unfortunate experience? Maybe she caught the vicar on an off-day? If he had understood the practical and spiritual problems she was grappling with, surely he would have been more concerned? Not necessarily so.

Remember Andrew, the clergyman who left his wife? His superiors could hardly fail to be aware of the dilemma in which he was placing himself and his family, yet the official church representatives were so cold and clinical it was unbelievable. All they wanted was to get him out of the way as quickly and quietly as possible.

In fact, the higher the position of responsibility a person had in the Church the harsher the treatment he seemed to receive. One Free Church member was forced to resign from all positions of leadership in his local church. Yet he felt the church people had been instrumental in the marriage breaking up. 'Had they handled it differently,' he explained, 'I'm pretty certain there would have been no divorce. Had they said, "We will not take sides, we do not know the full story, we will offer pastoral care to both, we will counsel both," then maybe we would still be together.'

Of course the Church has a responsibility to ensure that its leaders are not 'blind leaders of the blind' but the great men of the scriptures were not always infallible. Moses was a murderer. Paul consented to murder. David was an adulterer – but repentance was followed by forgiveness and a new dedication to God's service. Are we to be more strict than God in our judgements?

Happily there are some fellowships seeking to understand and share in the hurt and healing of their members. Several of the younger, unsupported mothers had found practical help and friendship through pram clubs and social activities organised by the Church. Others valued the counsel and prayer support they were offered, or the companionship of shared meals and homes. Someone whose confidence and self-respect have been shattered by the break-up of a marriage can find it is an enormous relief to discover that 'people accept you for what you are, rather than what you feel – a big failure.'

Talking to other Christians
We are back to the dreaded word failure again, but it was in their relationship with God and other Christians that people experienced this feeling most acutely. Mike described it as going through a spiritual wilderness; others felt they had been deserted by God, or failed God. This feeling was accentuated and drove people into a defensive position when so-called Christians started to judge, without adequate or reliable knowledge.

One Free Church minister learnt from his mistakes when he failed to prevent a congregation taking sides in a divorce case. Now he would make sure any counselling was submitted to the judgement of God and the scriptures, and would strongly urge that no member should be left to bear the pain of divorce alone.

'I feel we should be able to cope with the problems together if we are really members of the body of Christ, belonging to one another,' he said. 'The hurt of one is the hurt of all. The joy of one is the joy of all. We turn up for the weddings. The pain should be shared too. In the Christian community we're not yet able to tackle this whole area openly enough to be of help. Therefore any injection into our thinking and educational programmes which will make us more aware might teach us to be the kind of caring, loving community Christ wants us to be.'

We may have a long way to go before such an ideal can be achieved, but there does seem to be a growing concern within many branches of the Church that Christians should be more aware of how deep-rooted some emotional and psychological problems are. An article in the *Church of England Newspaper* in February 1979 was headed *When a little talk with Jesus doesn't make it right, all right*. It outlined the work of Care and Counsel, one of a number of centres attempting to assist the Church in its pastoral ministry through seminars, research, training programmes and personal counselling.

Talking to an experienced counsellor
The very idea of going for counselling can be daunting. Counselling agencies are not always easy to find (see lists on pages 127–130) and prices vary considerably. Some agencies charge a set fee and can be very expensive, others encourage clients to contribute what they can afford, so it is always wise to inquire about costs before booking an appointment.

A major hurdle for someone with an urgent matrimonial problem is the fact that they may have to wait anything from two to six weeks for an interview, and always there is the fear of the unknown. What kind of questions will they ask? Will it be all middle-aged ladies in tweeds? What if they tell you it's your fault? A fear commonly expressed is that counsellors are only interested in preserving marriage, but emphasis is now being placed on the need to counsel people *through* a divorce – if that is their decided course of action. 'Usually we try to help people explore their problems in a systematic and courageous way,' a counsellor explained. 'Then they look at the options open to them, and make their own decisions. They'll do that anyway. One reason for not giving specific advice is that people don't usually take it. You just help people to see what they really want or need.'

Apparently a lot of people say their marriage has finished when they're really asking if it could continue. Several divorced people expressed regret that they had gone ahead with divorce proceedings without really considering the alternatives. Go to a third party, somebody outside the immediate scene, out of the battlefield, somebody who will act as referee, they urged, particularly if you are in danger of making a rash or hasty decision. Here a note of regret often crept into the conversation; if only we had done nothing for a year . . . if only my wife would have come for counselling . . . if only I hadn't agreed to a divorce quite so easily.

One of the biggest problems counsellors have to face is the partner who will *not* come for counselling. By talking to one partner the marriage may still be helped, but the ideal is to see both. Then both viewpoints can be heard and, hopefully, brought together. One woman had been very reluctant to go for counselling, but afterwards she was relieved that her husband had insisted she must. 'You get something off your chest you've been wanting to say for ages,' she explained. 'You can talk about things you wouldn't dream of saying to anybody else. You don't get the feeling they're thinking "Hurry up and go home. All you want to talk about is your troubles." They're there to help you with your troubles.'

Unfortunately as the number of divorces increases, counselling agencies are finding great difficulty in coping with the people who need help. One remedy could be that those who express concern about the breakdown of marriage and family life should put themselves forward for training as counsellors. We may make the excuse that we are not qualified, but it is the kind of person you are that is important; whether you have degrees of empathy to listen and enter into another person's experience.

Even if we cannot train as counsellors we can still seek to have a better understanding of the emotional and practical upheavals created by divorce, so that when a friend or neighbour turns to us in their distress we are better equipped to cope. Only a minority of people with marital problems may actually get to the counselling agencies, but in many ways their very existence is an indictment on a society where people need to turn to a professional body before they can find someone who will listen and understand.

A word of warning
Whoever people turn to for advice, however, only the two partners in a marriage have ultimate power to decide whether it should end or continue.

'If I'd listened to my Mum in the beginning I wouldn't have had a marriage breakdown and a divorce,' Sam said. 'But when it comes to the crunch you've got to go by your own feelings and weigh up everything, what you think is for the best. Any decision you make in this world has got to be your own in the end. You can talk to a thousand people, or the wisest man in the world, but in the end it's still your decision.'

Questions for discussion or personal meditation

1. How important is it to bridge the 'communication gap' to help people share the things they have avoided? Are Christians honest and open enough to help in this task, or do we too often hide behind a barrier of spirituality, deceiving ourselves as well as others?
2. What practical steps are taken in your area to prepare couples for marriage, and to support them through the first five years (and afterwards)? Are they adequate? What else could be done? What could you do about it?
3. Why do you think those in a leadership position in the Church receive harsher treatment from their fellowship when their marriages break up, than those who come in from outside? How can we get a balance between the high standards we are led to expect of our leaders (1 Tim. 3.1–7) and the fact that no one is infallible (Rom. 3.23).
4. Should we share in the hurt and healing of our fellow Christians, or leave them to struggle through their spiritual and emotional wilderness unaided? Why?

6

The lesser of two evils

How do people make a decision when they are at a low ebb emotionally and mentally? What kind of thinking influences them? Do they consider all the implications?

A very real danger seems to lie in making a hasty decision, particularly if the partner has been deserted in favour of another companion. When she discovered her husband was having an affair with a younger woman, Carol's response was to rush to the solicitor with the idea of petitioning for divorce. Her solicitor had the wisdom to realise that she was not really capable of making such an important decision on the spur of the moment. He told her to wait a while, until she felt more adjusted to the situation. When she visited him a second time he could see that she had really thought about it. She had reached a decision which was less influenced by feelings of spite or wounded pride. Even so, she is still uncertain that she made the right decision and has gone through varying phases of wondering if the marriage could have continued.

'We had such a good marriage,' she said. 'It was a wretched shame ... for just one stupid infatuation.' Maybe you think Carol is a disillusioned woman, struggling along as a one-parent family, missing a familiar pillar to lean on? Not a bit of it. She has a beautiful home, is smart and independent, and has a very good finincial settlement. But the regret remains. Her conversation bristles with 'Ifs'.

Carol made sure that her financial and housing situation would be favourable before making an irrevocable decision. Others found themselves in a position where problems with housing and maintenance virtually forced them into divorce proceedings. Sandra was in a council flat which was in her husband's name. When he deserted her and the children she feared she would be made homeless. She reasoned if she petitioned for divorce she could also apply to have the tenancy of the home transferred to her name.

Another wife was abandoned with a young baby. Her husband periodically refused to pay maintenance. Every time she approached Social Security she had to repeat her story. Then one day they asked, 'What about the man you are living with?' She had taken more than enough. She knew she could not face that kind of humiliating questioning every time her husband was awkward, and decided there and then to apply for a divorce.

There is a popular fallacy that divorce is a soft option for people who do not take their commitment to marriage seriously enough. But the majority of people whose marriages have broken down find the decision to apply for divorce, or to allow proceedings to go ahead, painful and distressing. So many things have to be taken into consideration – finance, housing, children, the emotional upheaval. Only when they were pushed to the limit did divorce really become a serious consideration. Then they spoke of 'not being able to cope', 'of being at my wits' end'. or of 'not being able to go on for the rest of my life wondering who he was going off with next'.

Possible effect on the children
What if there were children involved? Couldn't the parents sink their differences and make some attempt to stay together for 'the sake of the children'? Did the parties consider the effect divorce might have on their children, materially and emotionally? The answer was a resounding 'yes'. Virtually everyone was 'aware of the problems', and tried to come to a decision that would result in the 'least possible damage'.

Many stayed together 'because of the children' until

they felt that was doing more harm than divorce would. Children quickly sense the tension that can exist between husband and wife, and use it to play off one parent against another, or feel torn between the two parents. Mrs Dee stayed with her partner longest, but found it was an uphill battle with Mr Dee 'working against her' all the time. In the end she knew she was faced with two alternatives – him or them.

Psychiatrists reckon that the children of battered parents are often very disturbed. Physical violence leaves such a lasting impression on young minds. One little girl remembered, 'Daddy pushing Mummy down the stairs', while another got the strap from whichever parent lost an argument. 'I felt like I was the centre-piece,' she explained. 'They were taking it out on me more than on themselves. When they split up I was told Dad was going away to work and I'd see him at week-ends. We had to move and I lost my friends and everything. I was completely bewildered. I felt very bitter. I'd got no love for either of them then. It's made me very hard.' Perhaps she illustrates most clearly the dilemma parents are faced with, when contemplating divorce. If her parents had stayed together she would have suf-fered. When they parted she still suffered.

Arbitrating between parent and child

Many parents do not have the ability to cope with their children's pain on top of their own grief. Courts and solicitors may negotiate material provision for the chil-dren, but who can arbitrate between child and parent when one is aggressive and the other sullen and with-drawn? Grandparents, godparents, aunts, uncles, older brothers and sisters, welfare officers, teachers, a good neighbour can all help to take the tension out of a poten-tially explosive situation, and help parents (and chil-dren) to see how far-reaching their actions and attitudes may be.

In July 1974 the Finer Report on one-parent families recommended the setting up of Family Courts, where the emphasis would be on conciliation and co-operation. Professionally trained staff would provide the 'missing link' between divorcing partners, their children, the social services, and the court. More recently, the Law Society produced a discussion paper entitled *A Better Way Out*, which again suggests that informal family courts should be established. So far, only the Bristol Courts Family Conciliation Service has got anywhere near implementing such ideas. There, social workers, solicitors, and marriage guidance counsellors work hand in hand to sort out the wrangles between divorcing partners.

Where there is continuing conflict between the parents about the children and their future, the need for a mediator, or conciliator, is desperate. Children are so much a part of ourselves it can never be easy to let them go, but what can happen when they are used as pawns between rival factions was brought home vividly to a schoolteacher in a small town.

When his wife left him she gave him an ultimatum. 'Agree to an undefended divorce petition and you can have custody.' He knew that she would be petitioning on grounds of cruelty. What would that do to his career, with reports splashed across the local papers or bandied from mouth to mouth? He could contest it, but to contest a divorce takes time and money, and the possibility of even more publicity. He reckoned the children had suffered enough. His own reputation and prospects were of secondary importance. He agreed to the divorce.

Pressure to agree to a divorce
Others underwent a less dramatic, but no less traumatic, form of blackmail, and once again it was the abandoned partner who suffered the most. With the threat that, because of the 1969 Divorce Reform Act, divorce proceedings could go ahead regardless of their opinion after five years' separation, few of them could resist the pressure to agree to a divorce after two years. Worries about finance, the children, and housing, combined with the shock of the partner leaving home and the

numbing effects of tablets, all lowered their resistance and left them less able to withstand the constant emotional pounding from a partner determined to get their own way. Many agreed to a divorce by the quickest method possible – then regretted it later. 'Looking back, I wish I had made him wait,' one woman sighed, 'not out of bitterness. I just have this feeling he might have come back again. He doesn't seem any happier with his new wife than he was with me.'

Few people would wish to see a return to the old system where a matrimonial offence had to be proved, or where one partner could create long-term havoc by refusing a divorce, but things now seem to be swinging to the opposite extreme. Since the 1969 Divorce Reform Act became law in January 1971, the 'irretrievable breakdown' of a marriage has been taken as the only ground for divorce. This can be proved in several ways:

1) adultery – if the partner finds it impossible to continue the relationship;
2) unreasonable behaviour – such that the petitioner cannot reasonably be expected to live with the respondent;
3) desertion (two years at least);
4) after two years' separation – if both partners agree (mutual consent);
5) after five years' separation – even if one partner does not consent.

But a recent pamphlet issued by the Law Society proposes one year separation as the sole evidence of the irretrievable breakdown of a marriage, even if one partner objects. It is suggested that such reform would get rid of many of the arguments between the partners, that divorce law should reflect the social attitudes of the times.

What did people think who had agreed to a 'quickie' divorce? They were the ones who expressed most regrets, and most hurt at the apparent ease in disposing of an unwanted partner. How will such people fare if the 'brake' is relaxed even further? Is one year long enough to make the far-reaching decisions that are necessary in divorce? If bereavement takes an average two years to accept, and divorce is a bereavement experience, how can the bereaved partner cope with an acceleration of the process? And why should the decision be taken completely out of the control of one party? What about the rights of the individual?

Jeff's divorce went through an American court where the separation period needed to be only six months. How did he feel about it? 'She filed for divorce ready or not, agreed or not, smiling or crying or however I felt,' he said. 'It was like death and taxation, something that could not be avoided.'

There are those who will insist that if a marriage has broken down, no amount of pleading by one partner can hold it together but it does seem that a number of people are accepting divorce because of what can only be described as emotional or psychological blackmail.

Questions for discussion or personal meditation

1. What factors need to be considered if someone is contemplating divorce? Is it an easy option? (Say why, or why not.)
2. What is the difference between conciliation and reconciliation? Why is there a need for people to act as conciliators in a divorce? What challenge does this present to Christians, in view of Jesus' teaching in Matthew 5.9?
3. Why are hasty decisions dangerous? How could you help someone resist the pressure to agree to a divorce too hastily? Do you agree that one year's separation should be the sole ground for the irretrievable breakdown of a marriage? (Say why, or why not.) What are you going to do about it?
4. What point is there in discussing alternatives, in view of Sam's comment, 'You can talk to a thousand people, or the wisest man in the world, but in the end it's still your decision'?
5. How would you cope with your own sense of inadequacy if you failed to prevent someone going ahead with a divorce?

7

Conflict of mind for Christians

One of the most distressing aspects of divorce is facing up to the fact that the promises made in marriage have been broken. Several people said they didn't believe in divorce, and described it as wrong, or bad. 'You make these vows in sincerity,' Becky explained, 'for better or for worse. You know then that there are the good times and the bad times. You stick with your partner. So it was against all I said I would do.'

If the promises have been made in Church, before God, by a sincere Christian, they are likely to be tormented by a great burden of guilt and failure. Becky felt that God was displeased with her decision to divorce, and with her as a person. She was not unique in her reactions. There is still a distinct feeling that divorce is wrong and a failure, even in our permissive society. Part of this is due to social pressure to conform and to the expectations that marriage will be for life, but another reason could be that a lot of our thinking and feeling about divorce is rooted in our Christian heritage.

Biblical principles
Traditionally the Church has based its teaching about marriage on the relationship between man and woman in the Creation stories. There God is depicted as making a suitable companion to help man. She is so much part and parcel of his existence that he is prepared to leave 'his father and mother and is united with his wife, and they become one'. (Gen. 2.21–24, GNB.) It was only later that the great leader, Moses, permitted divorce. (Deut. 24.1–4.) When the religious leaders of his day

questioned Jesus about divorce, hoping to trick him into an answer they could use against him, Jesus took them right back to basic principles. He conceded that Moses allowed divorce, but only because the people were so unteachable (or because of the hardness of their hearts).

'"But in the beginning, at the time of creation, God made them male and female,"' he reminded them. '"And for this reason a man will leave his father and mother . . . and the two will become one." So they are no longer two, but one. Man must not separate, then, what God has joined together.' (Mark 10.6–9, GNB.)

When pressed by his disciples about 'this matter' he further added, 'A man who divorces his wife and marries another woman commits adultery against his wife. In the same way, a woman who divorces her husband and marries another man commits adultery.' (Mark 10.10–12).

Practical application
How does the Church interpret this teaching today? The report, *Marriage and the Church's Task*, states: 'He (Jesus) was calling his hearers to get their basic idea of marriage straight. He intended his words to be taken with the utmost seriousness. Marriage is for life. Husband and wife form a new kind of unity. Divorce is as destructive of this unity as adultery.' p. 118.)

It is obvious that any Christian faced with divorce is going to experience enormous moral and spiritual conflict, trying to sort out just what the scriptures say and how they should be applied. Was Jesus forbidding divorce for time and eternity? Was he standing out against the lax divorce laws of his day and trying to shock people into realising the seriousness of the commitment they made in marriage? Is divorce permissible in some circumstances? How does the teaching in the Bible relate to my situation and the situation in my country today?

Some interpret the scriptures legalistically, insisting there should be no divorce. Basing their beliefs on the same scriptures, others maintain that divorce ought not to happen, but that it may 'sometimes be the only way forward in the situation that human sin and failure have created'. (*The Nottingham Statement* p. 65) A third opinion reluctantly concedes that divorce is permitted on the grounds of immorality (Matt 5.31,32) and desertion of an unbelieving partner (1 Cor. 7.15).

However they interpret scripture there is one point on which Christians are likely to agree. Divorce is not the ideal. Marriage is a covenant relationship which should not (some would say could not) be broken. In Ephesians 5.21–33 Paul compares the marriage relationship to that of Christ and his Church; a relationship based on love, respect, self-sacrifice, care and concern. With such an ideal before us it is hardly surprising Christians faced with a marriage breakdown are overwhelmed by a deep sense of failure and inadequacy.

Ideal and reality
Andrew, the Church of England vicar, had been forced to work through many such tensions when parishioners first started approaching him with marriage problems. Little did he realise he would be walking the same path himself one day. How did he reconcile theology and humanity?

'I think the scriptures are very realistic,' he replied. 'God's ideal for man was monogamy, but he permitted divorce. When Jesus spoke about Moses' provision for the "hardness of your heart" that was God acknowledging human frailty, so it's as if he's got his ideal in one hand and the reality in the other, and we move in the area in between. I accept divorce because I accept fallen humanity, and our own weakness, but that doesn't make me condone it, or wish it wasn't so. I would assert that our ultimate happiness lies in obeying God's ideal, rather than exploiting what he permits. Which means working on a marriage rather than giving up on it. I don't think the ideal is in scripture because it's something that suits God, but because it's our happiness that

51

God wills. I think we are made to receive more from monogamy than any other way in terms of sexual relationships, but love is one of our powerful emotions and it's easy to make a mistake in that area. It seems to me we allow forgiveness on proper contrition and penance ... for any sin under the sun, and yet we penalise people for making a mistake in their marriage.'

None of us find it easy to admit we have made a mistake, especially one we seem incapable of putting right. Those with the highest ideals and expectations find failure a particularly bitter pill to swallow. So Christians are unlikely to come through a marriage breakdown without lasting spiritual scars.

Many have been forced to re-think concepts they had accepted without question, others to examine themselves in an effort to discover where they have been responsible for the marriage breakdown. Sometimes this has led to a harsh awareness that they are selfish or escapist, that they don't know how to give, or forgive; painful discoveries, especially for a Christian. 'The bible does say forgive, doesn't it?' said Mrs Dee. 'We should forgive seventy times seven, but obviously I haven't forgiven him if I divorced him. Even now I get doubts. Should I have gone on, and let myself break down under the strain?' She knows there is a gap between the ideal and reality. She struggled to reconcile the two for twenty years. In the end she felt constrained to accept the 'lesser of two evils' or 'second best'.

Psychological barriers
Her inner conflicts still manifest themselves in varying physical forms. Others were so burdened by their sense of guilt and failure they suffered depression, or neared breakdown point, particularly if their low self-image was reinforced by harsh or unthinking judgements from those around them. One man was tied up in so many spiritual knots he alternated between four-hour drinking bouts and four-hour sessions of prayer. Another felt he was an outcast from the church fellowship, and tended to assume any adverse reactions on the part of

his fellow Christians were directly related to his divorce.

Some believed the broken relationship could and should have been put right. But they felt hopelessly inadequate to cope with the situation and nobody else seemed bothered enough to help, so they decided to 'blow theology' or opt out of the Church completely. Mike summed up the feeling of a lot of people when he said, 'She walked out. She asked to come back, then changed her mind. I am still prepared to accept her back but if she wants a divorce then that's her decision.'

Spineless? Defeatist? Unchristian? Mike is well aware of the accusations that can, and have been levelled against him. He acknowledges if he really cared about the marriage he would have taken more positive action. He might say he wanted his wife back, but his wife wasn't convinced, and his friends thought he looked relieved when she went. 'Perhaps what I did or didn't do, shows my attitude towards the marriage more than anything I've ever said,' he admitted. 'The fact that she had gone meant the tension was temporarily alleviated, and it took the conflict out of my mind. She put me in a situation where I was not morally responsible any more.' How far it is possible to abdicate responsibility is open to question, but it seems a popular option when people are unable to cope with the situation. For it is those with the highest ideals or strongest convictions who often find most difficulty in forgiving themselves, or believing that God can forgive them either.

Certain branches of the Church are now beginning to recognise the burden of guilt carried by those whose marriages have broken down, and have compiled a service where divorced believers may express their penitence and seek release from their vows. Others demonstrate God's love and forgiveness through their care and acceptance of his repentant sons and daughters. But some still cling to the belief that divorce 'doesn't happen to Christians', so when it does the divorcees are judged as 'second class' or 'inferior' or not 'real Christians'. This can mean that Christians are afraid to admit there are problems in their marriage, so the situation escalates.

Andrew took two years to pluck up courage to leave his wife, although the relationship had been shaky for more than a decade. He did once walk out in the middle of a row but appeared as usual on Sunday so that his parishioners didn't know. When he did eventually leave her, people quickly – and wrongly – jumped to the conclusion that his wife was to blame, and he has had to be 'prepared to take a lot of stick for the sake of the greater good'.

Particular problems of clergy
In fact, clergy and their wives are in a particularly difficult situation when their marriage breaks down. Who can they talk to? In some areas pastoral counselling centres have been established where people can discuss their problems with counsellors who would have a special awareness of the specific conflicts experienced by Christians. But all too often, like Marriage Guidance, these may be staffed by fellow colleagues.

The Church hierarchy theoretically have pastoral oversight of their staff and they would seem an obvious possibility. But as one clergy wife pointed out, 'That seems disloyal. They're the husbands' bosses. A teacher's wife wouldn't go and talk to the headmaster about her husband, or a worker to his managing director.' She suggested that clergy consider going for counselling out of their immediate area. But that may cost money, and money is a sore point for clergy and those in control of the diocesan purse strings. Another possibility is for each diocese to appoint an adviser on marriage problems. One thing is certain, with an increase in the number of clergy marriages breaking down, something needs to be done – and soon.

Annulment procedures
The Roman Catholics may not have problems about divorce and re-marriage as far as their priests are concerned, but the problems are none the less real for their people. One way out of the dilemma they have sought

has been through the extension of the annulment procedures. Historically annulment has been possible if it can be proved there was an intent not to have children, or to regard the marriage as anything less than permanent or exclusive. Recently, however, the grounds for nullity have been extended to cover ignorance of the nature of marriage, inability to fulfil the obligations of marriage and lack of due discretion. The Catholics argue that if there was something basic lacking in the relationship then the marriage can be declared 'null and void'.

It has been suggested that the Anglican church should consider extending their understanding of annulment but the Lichfield Report rejected the suggestion, preferring to see developments in pastoral care rather than in legal procedure. Apart from the obvious practical difficulties of administration, concern was voiced about the problems that could arise in defining maturity and immaturity and in declaring a marriage of many years invalid.

Becky, whose marriage is currently before the Catholic Marriage Tribunal, also expressed doubts. She found it incredible that although she knew, and the people round her knew, her marriage had happened, a piece of paper could say that was not the case. She felt it would be better to admit that it did happen, but it was a mistake which she regretted. 'Nobody goes around doing everything right, do they,' she asked. 'Even murderers can be forgiven. They can have their life sentence commuted to so many years. I don't feel like a criminal though, even if the Church makes me feel like one.'

So great was her distress and perplexity she sought counsel from a number of priests. She felt they were sympathetic but powerless to suggest anything other than that she should try for an annulment. She is hoping that eventually a declaration of nullity will relieve her spiritual conflict but for the present it only seems to be prolonging the agony, as sworn statements from witnesses, the preparation of documents, the formal hearing and the right to appeal against any decision all involve time, money, and the re-opening of old wounds.

Condemnation or compassion

It seems strange that so often people particularly in need of love and acceptance find condemnation rather than compassion from all branches of the Christian Church. Recognising the tension there is between 'the demand and compassion of our Lord', and 'the actualities of married life and love given human weakness and sin', the Lichfield Report suggests that 'the task facing the Church is to fashion a discipline which holds before those who are married, and those about to marry, the challenge of unconditional love, while offering to those who have failed in their marriage, the possibility of a new beginning.' (p. 266.)

Some of the practical suggestions for exercising pastoral care and compassion include making people aware of the need for support during the problematic first five years of marriage and the shock of parenthood. It stresses that this is an area where the whole family of God can be involved by organising pram clubs, playgroups, baby-sitting, marriage enrichment groups, and simply befriending people.

Indeed it could be something as simple as befriending which holds some hope for those hurt by a broken marriage, or a marriage at risk. Invaluable as the work of the counselling agencies may be, only a small percentage of people actually cross their thresholds. It is to their friends and neighbours that folk turn in their time of distress. This is a challenge to each of us to be aware of the problems, willing to listen with understanding and compassion, quick to offer practical help and support, but slow to make hasty judgements or to think we have the power or the right to decide anyone else's future for them.

Questions for discussion or personal meditation

1. What particular conflicts do Christians experience when faced with a marriage breakdown? Why?

2. Is it possible to reconcile the ideal and the reality? (Say why, or why not.) Give scriptural and practical justification.

3. How do you feel when you know you fall short of God's ideal?
   a) Can you forgive yourself?
   b) Do you believe God forgives you?
   c) Can you forgive others their faults?
   d) Could you help someone else understand and accept God's forgiveness?

4. Is divorce the 'unforgivable sin'? Why do people going through a marriage break-up often feel that it is?

5. Does offering care and compassion mean you condone divorce? Is condemnation likely to alter or harden people's attitudes?

8

Trying for reconciliation

If anxiety is related to uncertainty it might be supposed that once a decision has been made there would be a temporary sence of relief. Unfortunately human emotions are not that predictable, and even the most decisive person can be subject to agonies of doubt. Several people spoke of 'varying phases' of wondering if they might get back together, particularly in the early days of the marriage break-up. 'You are torn,' explained one wife. 'Half of me regrets agreeing to a divorce, and half of me doesn't. It's an awful struggle ... like being in limbo.'

It is at this stage people seem most open to help – if only there was someone who cared enough to become involved. The injured feelings which have led to the threat of divorce are often giving way to grim realisation that life alone, or as a one-parent family, might well be more difficult than fighting to preserve the marriage.

A first priority
The Christian Gospel is one of reconciliation and forgiveness, so many ministers will refuse to discuss divorce until they have first discussed marriage and reconciliation. Similarly the 1969 Divorce Reform Act was formulated with an eye to reconciliation, and solicitors are required to discuss this possibility and give names and addresses of agencies able to advise and counsel. 'We get a lot of people phoning up at 9 a.m. on Monday morning screaming blue murder, 'explained one solicitor, 'but when I actually sit them down and we talk about the implications of divorce, it seems to fizzle out. In about half the cases that's the last I ever hear.'

Sadly, though, in many cases reconciliation was only

mentioned in passing, and in others it was not even considered. Andrew, the clergyman, was particularly bothered that in spite of the support he received from his solicitor, reconciliation was not encouraged. Yet in his job that possibility was foremost in people's minds.

It's never too late

Reconciliation remains a possibility until the granting of the decree absolute (the legal documents terminating the marriage which are issued six weeks after the court proceedings). Until then it is never too late to make an attempt to save the situation. But who will make the first move? Wounded pride may prevent the parties involved giving way, only a small proportion of people actually consult someone who can really help, solicitors often ignore the possibility of reconciliation, doctors are more likely to prescribe tablets than let the patient talk about their problems. Once again the onus seems to fall fairly and squarely on the friends and family. But how do you intervene in something as personal as a marriage break-up without making the situation worse? 'The first thing is to look to see if there is some means whereby with changed attitudes and deeper understanding of the problems there might be a possibility of restoring the relationship and rebuilding,' a doctor suggested. '*You* can't change people's attitudes but if you can help them see *why* they feel angry or resentful or bitter, or where their attitudes may have been wrong, that may be the first stage towards a reconciliation.'

A Baptist pastor, convinced of the need for urgent action in the early stages of a marriage breakdown, spoke of driving many miles and sitting up through the night more than once in an attempt to reconcile opposing partners. He believes that if the Church is responsible for marrying people they should be 'in the business of reconciliation – at all costs.'

Counting the cost

There is a danger, though, that counsellors might press for a reconciliation regardless of the fact that the 'cost' has to be borne by the couple concerned, and not by the counsellor.

Reconciliation may well be a viable alternative to divorce, but the doubts and fear of further hurt are never far beneath the surface. One wife didn't really want a divorce and was quite open to the possibility of reconciliation, but she still wasn't sure how far her 'love could stretch'. Could she and her husband overcome their differences? Would they ever be able to fully trust one another again? What would happen next time they came up against a crisis? On one side there was the pleasant picture of a happy marriage as she knew it could be; on the other, the nightmare of some of the worst moments.

Re-entering the conflict
Despite all the odds against it, return and restoration *are* possible, even after years of disunity and misunderstanding. (See Alan and Margaret Havard's book *Death and rebirth of a marriage*.) The Holy Spirit can intervene to change lives and attitudes, however unlikely it may seem.

One of Jesus' parables describes the foolishness of the person who sets out to build a tower without estimating whether he can afford to finish it. Hopefully, when people begin to realise the real cost of divorce they will think more carefully about their relationships. One woman whose parents had divorced, seriously considered leaving her husband, until she thought of the consequences. 'I don't want my kids to have a life like I had,' she said. 'So I must try again.'

Combining the interests, needs and rights of two individuals has never been an easy task, even when marriage has all the authority of the Church and State to ensure its stability. How much more difficult it must be when roles and relationships are continually adapting and changing, and the temptation to opt out appears so much more attractive. 'It's very easy to have an affair,' mourned Barbara. 'It's much harder to stay happily married. You've got to work at it. It's not the divorce laws that should be changed. It's our attitude to marriage.'

Working at a marriage relationship is bound to involve sacrificing certain rights and interests once in a while. It could mean old values and judgements will have to be reassessed. It may involve fighting tooth and nail to preserve the identity of the individual inside the relationship, or to rescue a marriage that is drifting into danger. It will certainly require a good deal of thought and forethought as unpleasant realities are faced. Marriage can be an uphill battle for the most devoted couple. To enter the conflict a second time *knowing* the pathway will not be strewn with roses must take a considerable amount of courage and determination.

Mike and his wife, Madeleine, went into long discussions about the possibility of her returning home, and how they would cope if she did. Eventually Madeleine rang to ask if she might return the following weekend. Mike agreed apprehensively. The weekend arrived, and Madeleine decided not to return. 'That shattered me more than when she went in the first place,' Mike said. 'I didn't tell many people about that.' If partners did return and hopes were revitalised, people were left in a worse state when they departed a second time. 'You get used to being alone. You accept that they've gone, and when they come back you think everything will be all right,' explained Sandra. 'Then you're hurt all over again. You feel used.'

Broken promises and shattered dreams are hard to cope with but few outsiders appreciate the daily struggle and sacrifice that may be involved in 'getting together' again. It is only to be hoped that those who advise a reconciliation exert an equal amount of energy in supporting the couple if they encounter further problems. Unfortunately once a couple are reunited most people assume they have fulfilled their duty. All too often the couple are left to their own devices and it is not long before the same mistakes are being repeated. 'We did try,' the couple wail, shaking their heads as they attempt to come to terms with a second dose of bewilderment and hurt.

Mrs Dee tried – for twenty years only to be told by the minister who had most strongly urged a reconciliation he wasn't really surprised when the marriage split up. When the judge asked why she wouldn't take Mr Dee back, seeing she had already given him one chance, he received a curt reply. 'I said I professed to be a Christian and I thought I had to give him a chance,' she said. 'But after years of living with him I felt he was never going to be any different.'

According to Jack Dominian, a psychiatrist and medical adviser to the Catholic Marriage Advisory Council, the success of marital reconciliation depends on whether the partners are willing and able to change sufficiently to meet each others' *minimum needs*. Some obviously do, or marriage counsellors, clergy, and all in the 'business of reconciliation' would give up in despair. Others try until they are worn out with the effort. One girl felt it was asking too much of people to struggle on unaided. From her own experience, and that of her friends, she felt 'outside of God you just can't find a way to put the pieces back together.'

Going the second mile
Some would argue that even with God's help the going can be pretty tough. An RE teacher in a secondary school described how he persisted in contacting his wife regularly when she left home, even though at first she wanted nothing to do with him. Advisers declared he was stupid. He would compromise the separation and prolong divorce proceedings. He retaliated by pointing out that the relationship could only be restored if there were no barriers between them. After a few months his patience was rewarded, and he and his wife almost got to the point of putting the marriage back together. Now he is less optimistic about the future, but still prepared to persevere. Wasn't he putting himself in a vulnerable position? Didn't the old wounds re-open every time he was rebuffed?

'It's like going through torture,' he replied. 'I don't

think she has any idea what it costs. Now I feel I may have to acquiesce to a divorce after the two-year separation. I don't want a divorce. I still love my wife, but I can't bring myself to play around with her life. I'd like her to feel that I've done all I can, that I've gone the second mile as may times as possible.'

In spite of the fears and forebodings, in spite of a double portion of failure and rejection, I met no one who regretted making a second attempt at their marriage. If nothing else they felt they had not given up without an effort. 'I'm glad I tried a second time,' explained Barbara. 'Otherwise to this day I could be thinking ... if ... if I'd forgiven him. I don't begrudge him the extra two years. I can live with myself now.'

Questions for discussion or personal meditation

1. Should reconciliation always be the first priority for the Christian? (Say why, or why not.) Do you know the names and addresses of counselling agencies, or competent people to whom you could refer someone having problems with their marriage? Are such details listed in your church? Should they be?
2. Think of a situation where you have needed to look inside yourself to see why you felt angry, or resentful or bitter.
   a) Was it easy to say why, or why not.)
   b) What helped you to change your attitudes?
   c) Could you share that experience with someone working through similar emotions?
3. What kind of support is someone working towards, or through, a reconciliation likely to need? Is reconciliation the end of the story? What other help may be needed?
4. Barbara said, 'It's not the divorce laws that should be changed. It's our attitude to marriage.' Do you agree?
   a) What can be done to strengthen people's understanding of marriage?
   b) What is your church/fellowship doing?
   c) Do you need to work at your marriage? Why? How?

9

Help during divorce proceedings

Unfortunately, attempts at reconciliation often do not succeed. Things have gone too far and trying to restore the relationship is just 'not on'. This is just the time when help is needed, so that the situation is accepted and life can be looked at from a positive point of view. There are so many traumas associated with the actual divorce proceedings and a sympathetic friend or counsellor can do much to help ease them.

For those inside the system divorce is a complex affair, involving great tomes of reference several inches thick, and tapes to keep abreast with current changes in family law. What hope has the outsider of understanding anything other than basic details? Even the terminology used is like speaking a foreign language. Books such as the comprehensive *Which?* report, *On Getting Divorced*, need to contain a glossary explaining words like 'affidavit', 'cross petitions', 'injunctions', 'respondent' and 'co-respondent'. How do people with little or no legal knowledge feel about becoming entangled in a thing they do not fully comprehend?

Going to a solicitor
'I was scared about going to the solicitor,' said Sandra. 'It's an awful experience because you don't know what to expect. In some ways it's a bit like going to the dentist. I worried about what I'd have to say to him. I thought it would be the same as visiting Social Security, but his attitude was different. He was impartial.'

Once they had got over their initial timidity, the majority of people were delighted to find that solicitors were not a breed apart. With a few unpleasant exceptions, who seemed to be in business mainly for the money, solicitors encouraged the open sharing of problems and people respected the recommendations and advice they were given.

'If someone came into the office saying they wanted a divorce, the first thing I would try to do would be to find out why,' explained a young solicitor. 'Just to say, "Fill in a few forms and you'll be divorced in three and a half months' time" can be a disaster. I consider it important to respond to the situation almost as a counsellor, or an adviser, with certain legal skills. I sit and talk to them for about an hour about basic details like when they got married, the name of the spouse, number of children, and so on. I try to find out what's gone wrong, and what my client wants to see out of the situation. We sort out the three or four most likely possibilities for the future and if the client is still saying "I want a divorce", and I agree that seems to be the most appropriate action, I will go through all the information I need for the divorce petition and explain the basic machinery. Then I would say, "Think about it and phone me if you still want to go ahead." I try to avoid rushing clients into making a decision before they have time to digest all the legal and practical information.'

A lot of solicitors will actually fill in the forms for clients, rather than have endless correspondence correcting mistakes and nowadays, in an undefended divorce under the special procedure, a divorce can be obtained without either party appearing in court. For more complicated cases, or when children are involved, an appearance in court is usually necessary however; a thought that can be even more harrowing than a visit to the solicitor.

Going to court

The actual proceedings may take only a couple of minutes but the simple fact of having to appear in court at all can be enough to unnerve even the most hardy individuals. Behind the bravest exterior all kinds of fears may be lurking.

'I had to have tablets for the actual day,' said Mrs Dee. 'I didn't sleep for nights worrying about what they'd ask, and if I'd know the right words to answer. It's a funny feeling while you're waiting, kind of "now or never". You get a false courage. There was a great fear in my mind that I wouldn't get the divorce. In fact when I stood in the witness box and the judge said "decree nisi" I just couldn't take it in. I nearly got run over afterwards. I was so relieved I couldn't think.'

Those who didn't really want a divorce in the first place found the whole process particularly trying. Mrs Dee was not alone in needing tablets to carry her through the day. Solicitors may be around to give advice and support if there are likely to be any complications, but nowadays a number of people are not represented in court and are genuinely grateful for the moral support a friend can provide. Often the buildings are bleak and imposing, and the whole atmosphere sordid and depressing, so a companion, or a book, can help to relieve the tension, pass the time, and preserve some element of sanity.

Having to sit and listen to other cases is a distressing experience for those in a fairly emotional state. 'I had looked forward to married life,' explained one man. 'To go to court and see all types, some in tears, some blasé, women with tarty friends, others heartbroken, and a jovial solicitor guffawing, "Now you're free to go and do the same thing again," was squalid. It demeaned marriage. I felt very dirty when I came away and physically sick.'

Many people described going to court as upsetting, or distressing, some because they had not fully worked through their own feelings about divorce. For others, it was because of the grief or apparent indifference of those around them. Laughter can be a defence mechanism, or a camouflage. One woman deliberately chose a 'jolly' friend to accompany her, because she knew it would be a very heavy burden to stand up in court and say she no longer wanted her husband, when in fact she did.

When the official papers arrive

Now that fewer people are required to attend court, the reality of the situation may only strike home when the official papers arrive. Even those attending court could be numbed with a false security by tablets, so that the whole episode passed 'in a dream'. People might cope with the formal hearing, only to find themselves 'cracking up' unexpectedly when the decree absolute arrived.

Mike described how he had to walk to work the day his copy of the divorce petition landed on the doormat. Seeing things in black and white was such a shock he knew he couldn't concentrate on driving. How did he cope when the decree absolute arrived? 'I survived,' he said, 'with help from my friends, but I did get depressed afterwards.'

Experienced counsellors liken the arrival of the decree absolute to the effect of a funeral, and as with death it is a great mistake to assume that the major obstacles have been overcome once the public ritual has been observed. In reality the 'bereaved' person may only just be awakening to the full extent of their loss – a warning for all concerned about the welfare of their divorced friends or relatives.

Questions for discussion or personal meditation

1. Remember an experience you were apprehensive about – starting a new school, a new job, your wedding day, going to hospital.
   a) How did you cope with your fears?
   b) Were you able to discuss them?
   c) How did you keep your mind occupied while you were waiting?
   d) How did you feel afterwards?
2. If a friend or relative asked you to accompany them to court or to the solicitor's, would you be distressed at the thought of becoming involved in something unpleasant? Would that deter you, or give you a greater understanding of how your friend must be feeling?

10

Needs of the children

One of the main reasons for the anxiety connected with court appearances was the fear of what would be decided concerning the children. Three-quarters of all divorce cases involve children. A decree absolute cannot be granted until the judge is satisfied about the future of the children and has issued a 'Section 41 certificate'.

All too often the children are reluctant participants in a conflict which is beyond their comprehension, but parents may be equally bewildered about what really is 'best for the child'. Most parents have strong emotional and physical ties with their offspring and it cannot be easy to accept that a court has power to decide that one parent should have the day-to-day care of the children while the other can only enjoy their company at set times or under certain conditions. So how can parents come to an 'amicable agreement' about custody and access when they may barely be on speaking terms, or negotiating only through a solicitor?

Deciding custody
Where a parent has deserted the family there is usually 'no question' over which parent has custody. The parent already caring for the child, or children, normally continues to assume responsibility. Similarly, custody is unlikely to be contested where there are practical difficulties such as inadequate accommodation, or work which would involve considerable absence from home.

The age of the child is another important factor. It is generally agreed that very young children need their mother to care for their developing physical and emotional needs, and in many cases fathers would simply not know how to cope with the demands of a young child. There is a growing feeling, however, that there should be a fairer system of deciding custody and access, and a new pressure group 'Families need Fathers' is demanding that fathers should receive copies of school reports and other things likely to affect their child's future.

With the increase of labour-saving gadgets in the home, however, and fathers sharing more in the upbringing of their children, it is no longer automatically assumed that the mother is the best person to have custody. If a father can prove that he can make suitable arrangements for the children, or that the mother is not a fit person to look after them, a decision may be made in his favour. Where a third party is involved, the children will not be given to the 'injured party' purely as a reward for good behaviour. The future welfare of the child is always the deciding factor.

If there is a major disagreement about custody it is important for parents to be made aware of the long-term effects a protracted dispute could have on the children. Adults may be answerable for themselves, but their actions and attitudes can affect the future educational, emotional, psychological and social well-being of their children. Unhappily, parents may ignore this fact and children can be used as pawns in the matrimonial dispute. In extreme cases ridiculous claims can be made for custody. Mrs Dee's husband was in prison when their divorce came before the courts yet he applied for custody of the children. The solicitor tried to assure Mrs Dee that no court in the country would agree to his request. She was not convinced, and had no rest until the custody arrangements were signed and sealed.

The most harrowing cases are the prolonged custody battles which can continue for a number of months or years, and the most unhappy children of divorce are those torn between two parents unable, or unwilling, to see the havoc they are wreaking in the child's life. If opposing legal decisions are made in two different countries the conflict can be enormously costly. Large sums of money may be paid to private investigators willing to engineer a 'snatch', but the real cost is borne by the child torn between two selfish adults incapable of estimating the damage they are inflicting.

Unfortunately kidnapping appears to be on the increase, but an international treaty is now being drawn up to tighten the laws and cut through some of the red tape facing parents trying to regain their children. The Salvation Army Missing Persons Department (address on page 130) may be able to help in cases where parents are unable to trace their children.

An article about child snatching in *The Daily Telegraph* of 11 July 1979 described how a consultant in child psychiatry is convinced that 'there are no circumstances which justify child snatching. Parents who do so are motivated either by revenge or their own selfish needs; they see the child as another possession and have little or no consideration or understanding of his wants.'

Effects of parents' relationship

Traditionally teachers, psychiatrists and social workers have stressed the importance of a stable home background and the adverse effects on a child if they are deprived of one or both parents. Anger and resentment may be expressed towards the parent they feel has betrayed them, and to the remaining parent. If the child has been consciously, or unconsciously, aggravating the conflict between the parents, or been blamed for various rows or arguments, he or she may suffer agonies of guilt. When a parent, in a moment of temper or irritability, rounds on them with the comment, 'It's all your fault', their worst fears are confirmed.

'We took a lot of time to explain to the girls what was happening,' said one father, 'even though they were quite young. We told them we weren't happy; that this sometimes happens with married people, and it was hurting both of us. They obviously couldn't see it then, but we tried to explain so that they would understand as

70

they grew older ... and we *keep on* explaining it was because of the failure of *our* relationship, and not because of them.'

Children may be able to vent their emotions more freely in tears and tantrums, but the very fact that they cannot understand their grief must make it doubly hard to bear. If the parent fails to understand why they are behaving so 'unreasonably' and punishes them unjustly, they may withdraw into a private world of hostility and apparent indifference. In reality the parent should be concerned if children suppress their grief, for that is more likely to hinder the normal development of their personality. Research has indicated that a deterioration in school work, delinquency, bed-wetting, suicide attempts in later life and emotional and psychological disorders can all be linked to the loss of a parent through death or divorce.

In more recent years a growing number of people researching into the effects of divorce have been coming to the conclusion that 'emotional' divorce (that is, a broken relationship *within* the marriage) can cause more upset than actual physical divorce. In other words, children are disturbed when the relationship between their parents is disturbed. So a child from an unhappy marriage could suffer more adverse effects than the child in a divorce where the parents are able to maintain a relatively 'civilised' relationship'

Few children would recognise that their parents' problems were a direct cause of their stomach pains, or truancy, but parents are equally unwilling to admit that their child's behaviour problems can be a reflection of their marital breakdown. Child guidance clinics in a number of areas now insist on seeing the entire family, in the hope that parents may be helped to see how their relationship is affecting the child.

Much research is still needed in this whole area, but it does seem vital that children should be protected from the hostility that can exist between partners in a divorce case. Where parents were bitter and resentful towards their previous partner it was obvious that the children were quick to pick up the 'vibes', and express their own resentment in behaviour problems, or hostility towards one or both parents.

Young children can be particularly bewildered if they are 'used' by one parent to 'play off', or blackmail, the other. Mrs Dee remembered her five-year-old's confusion when his father waylaid him with a box of chocolates 'for Mummy' along with the message, 'Daddy still loves you. Why won't you let him come home?'

Explaining to the children

One thing psychiatrists, counsellors, divorcees and the children of divorced parents do agree on is the importance of explaining to the children what is happening when a marriage breaks up. But how can you explain the depth of the thinking that goes into such an important decision? You probably can't but you can answer their questions as honestly and fairly as possible, so that the children are not left completely in the dark.

However 'rational' the decision to part may appear to an adult, children may not be able to see things in the same light – particularly if there has been a close relationship with the parent who has left home. Their reactions may be particularly violent.

'You try explaining to a four-year-old why Daddy's not here,' said one mother. 'We did try, but a lot of it he couldn't understand. We used to have tantrums, a foot through the door, hitting and kicking. It was always worse when we'd been out. I think coming into the house brought back memories. I didn't mind if it was his toys, but when it came to the furniture that was a different story. When his Dad leaves after visiting him we still have a little bit of trouble, but not quite so bad. I think he's beginning to understand more now.'

Explaining does seem to help the situation – providing the parent is able to overcome their own hurt sufficiently to give an unbiased account. Research indicates that a child needs *both* parents, even after divorce, and that there are less likely to be problems if the child

later in life they reproached her for not divorcing him much sooner.

Access

In such cases the children might want little more to do with the absent parent. In others the parents want nothing to do with one another, yet the children still need to know the love and affection of both. Can parents 'sink their differences' sufficiently to put the child's welfare first? Some can, even if it requires a superhuman effort. Their children were the ones who seemed to be suffering least as a result of their parents' estrangement.

The man who could speak with pride of his daughters' maturity and intelligence, and the good relationship he had with them, had been mainly concerned about the girls when his marriage broke up. In spite of 'communication problems' with two young females, and the presence of a step-dad, he had persevered in maintaining a regular contact over the years. In fact he and his wife had been so concerned about the girls that normal access arrangements had seemed superfluous. 'We just assumed that access would be bound by the normal laws of politeness,' he said.

Not everyone is capable of managing their arrangements as amicably as that however, and access can be a real 'thorn in the flesh'. One partner's interpretation of 'reasonable access' may be very different from the other's. In Barbara's case the husband wanted the children every weekend. She said every other weekend. Because they refused to speak to one another everything had to be negotiated in writing. Her solicitor wrote to his. He would photocopy the letter and send a copy to the husband. Then the whole process was reversed, and one question could take a month to answer.

Even when the arrangements have been legally negotiated, that may be only the beginning of troubles. Solicitors can arbitrate, partners agree, courts give their seal of approval, then the whole thing prove unworkable in practice. A father may have access to his pre-school children every Sunday afternoon, but what do you do with them when it's pouring with rain and the film at the local cinema has an 'X' certificate? How can you maintain a relationship with a young child you only see at irregular intervals, and who hardly remembers you? How do you cope with the aggression of a child returning from an outing with a parent he adores, and knows he won't see for another three weeks? How do you cope with your own emotions if the partner you still love calls to see the children every day before going 'home' to the 'other woman'?

'Don't argue about the children,' said one mother, who was finding it very hard to share her children with her ex-spouse and his girl friend. 'He's got to see them, even though you don't want him to. It absolutely tore me apart knowing *she* was looking after them. I hated it. But *they* didn't. You've got to swallow your pride. The fact that she probably sits with them on her knee. Grr! Yet when he comes round here every day that's not right either. I'm sure if the solicitor knew he wouldn't get away with it, but immediately I mention it to the children there's great hostility. So what do I do? Do I allow him to come into my home and act as normal to keep the children happy, or do I put it on the official line and turn the children against me?'

When the partner lives nearby and has ready access it may be abused but if access can only be arranged during school holidays there can be just as many problems. Different establishments have different routines, and adjusting from one set of rules to another can create all kinds of conflict. Bedtimes, eating habits, television and general discipline are particular battlegrounds. Barbara's children visit their father every holiday and she dreads the first few days when they return. They are always so discontented and aggressive. The grass is so much greener at Daddy's, where they are regarded as visitors, and have all kinds of treats and outings. 'At home they have treats on birthdays and in the holidays,' said Barbara. 'But you can't afford to keep doing "extra" things. We might have bacon and eggs for breakfast when we have visitors, but it's back to the cornflakes once they've gone.'

The first time children go away can be a great wrench, especially if the children are apprehensive. It is very easy to be over-protective, or possessive. Fortunately most families discovered that visits became progressively less fraught, as the children learnt to adapt to the different routines and standards. One set of children were delighted to discover they had two major holidays – one at the seaside with Mother, and a second abroad with Father. As far as they were concerned they were on to a good thing!

Another unexpected bonus of divorce is that when formal access arrangements have been worked out the father may find himself spending more time with his offspring. All too often in a normal family set-up Father may be engrossed in his work during the day, and either exhausted, or out, in the evening. When access commits him to entertaining his children on a regular basis he may actually discover he enjoys their company, and such forgotten delights as fishing, the circus and the funfair. Meanwhile Mother may make good use of the spare time at her disposal to arrange a visit to the hairdresser's, a shopping expedition, or a part-time job to supplement the family's income.

Presents

Money, or lack of it, is often a source of irritation in divorce. If the father showers the children with expensive gifts and then quibbles about maintenance payments it is not likely to be appreciated. Like many other mothers struggling to save a small amount each week towards the children's birthdays or Christmas, Barbara found the presents her husband gave them very hard to accept. 'I was jealous,' she said. 'The presents were so big I had to pray a lot about it. Then the Lord made me realise that their father was trying to buy their love, yet I had it for nothing. But that lesson took a long time to learn.'

From the children's point of view it is a lesson that must be learned – no matter how much it may seem like bribery to the parent. Birthdays or Christmas could be made or marred by whether the absent parent remembered, or bothered, to send a present or card. One mother was completely bewildered when she found her daughter sobbing her heart out on Christmas afternoon. 'That's nice,' she remarked, 'after all you've had.' Back came the reply. 'But I still haven't got my Daddy.' That child is now a married woman with children of her own, but she hasn't forgotten the hurt she felt when her father forgot her birthday. 'I've still got every card he sent me,' she said wryly. 'All three of them.'

Problems

Admitting to schoolfriends who seem to have the normal quota of mums and dads, that one parent is missing, is another painful process. Most children want to conform to the accepted pattern, and it is not uncommon to hear them explaining earnestly that Dad is 'away on business', or 'in the back garden', when they know very well that he is really living with his girl friend in a flat on the other side of town. But now that broken relationships are becoming so much part of the social scene, children are more than likely to find someone in their street or class in a similar situation, and find strength and comfort in their shared experience. Indeed teachers may find that a fair proportion of their class have mixed-up family backgrounds, and it is no longer safe to assume that all children are able to produce the standard piece of writing about 'my Mum', or 'my Dad'.

Because the majority of children find difficulty in accepting that their parents have split up, they may exert pressure to get them back together again. Young children may resort to actual physical manoeuvring to get the parents seated on the same settee, or devastate them with a simple but shattering question such as, 'Why don't you and Daddy live together any more?'

Even when a child is not quite so explicit in his desires, the longing for the parents to be reconciled may still play an important part in his dreams or fantasies. A woman whose parents have been separated for twenty-five years admitted that she still lies in bed at times wishing that her parents could get together again, and planning all the things they could do as a family.

Any alteration in a shaky agreement between two partners can create further problems. If the parent with care and control decides to move to another part of the country a whole new set of arrangements have to be made about access, and old hostilities simmering beneath the surface quickly reach boiling point.

When Barbara told her ex-husband she intended to move he was very indignant. What effect would the move have on the children, he wanted to know. Was it fair to alter their lives, expect them to adjust to new schools, new friends? When would he see them? 'I told him he had made a new life,' said Barbara, 'and if he had been that concerned about the children the divorce wouldn't have happened in the first place.'

Grandparents
Grandparents also stand to lose a great deal as the result of divorce proceedings, in spite of new laws incorporated in the Domestic Proceedings and Magistrates Courts Act, 1978, which allow grandparents the right to claim access to their grandchildren. If the family moves to another part of the country, or the parent they are living with proves hostile and obstructive, the law may be of little avail with children and grandparents left equally hurt and bewildered by the severing of yet another relationship.

Perhaps one of the most difficult conflicts parents have to resolve is the fear that the other parent may be trying to turn the child against them, and what the child may decide to do when they are old enough to choose between the two parents. Even when children know living with the other parent wasn't really practical, the idea may still be there at the back of their minds to be used as a threat, or a daydream when reality becomes unpleasant.

'I shall tell Daddy of you,' can be a very effective weapon, especially if it is backed up with a further threat, 'And I shall go to live with him when I am old enough.' Barbara decided the only way to counter the attack was to call her daughter's bluff. 'I felt I was being blackmailed by a twelve-year-old,' she said, 'and that was ridiculous. So one day I offered her paper and pen while I dictated a letter as to *why* I was telling her off.'

This problem can be accentuated as the child moves through teenage, especially if they never have become reconciled to the fact that the parent they once loved has abandoned them, or if there is considerable friction with the remaining parent or step-parent. In one sense all the parent can do is stand back and hope the child will not make a decision which will only lead to further hurt and disappointment, just as the parent of an adopted child can only watch apprehensively if the child arranges to meet the original mum. 'The boy will go away occasionally with his Dad,' one mother said reluctantly. 'I'm not too happy about that. Perhaps I'm frightened he'll want to stay with him. I think it would really shake me if he went to live with him after I'd struggled to bring him up.'

That mother had the sense to realise that her fears must remain hidden from the child. To resort to tears, or try to turn the child against his father would only be counter-productive. Children are not fools. They may threaten, or actually walk out in a fit of temper, but if there is real security and love underneath the surface tensions they will soon come sneaking back home.

Janet's marriage split up ten years ago. Janet and her daughter were relieved that the husband and his violent temper were no longer part of the domestic scene. The son found it harder to accept the fact that his father had gone. When a stepfather moved in the son moved out – to live with his real father. Janet worried. But what could she do? She waited.

'The conditions he was living in were indescribable,' she said. 'But then he started to pop in home – for a meal, or things to be washed. First it was once a week, then every other day. But he couldn't bring himself to ask if he could come back for good. That was left to me. He didn't take much persuading though. He soon had his bags packed and was back at base. I expect we'll have our differences. We always have. But at least he knows now where he's really wanted.'

Questions for discussion or personal meditation

1. What effects could divorce, or a disturbed relationship between parents, have on a child? Is staying together because of the children necessarily a good thing? (Say why, or why not.)
2. Why bother trying to explain to a child if they are too young to understand? What particularly needs explaining? Why?
3. Think of a time when you have had to share a friend or a member of your family with someone else.
   a) What emotions did you experience?
   b) What practical problems were there?
   c) What areas of your life do you find difficulty in sharing now? Why?
   d) How can you best help someone who is finding great difficulty accepting custody and access arrangements?
   e) Could you encourage them to see the other person's point of view, and help them to work through their fears and jealousies?

11

One-parent families

Access may present recurring problems for both parents, but the parent with care and control of the child is likely to be more concerned about the day-to-day headache of coping as a lone parent. One in nine of all families in Great Britain is now a one-parent family and more than one and a quarter million children are being brought up by one parent coping alone. Rearing children is not the easiest of tasks with the support and aid of a partner, so how does one parent manage unassisted? What are the special problems they find themselves facing?

Poverty, or at least a lowering in the standard of living, is the first obvious practical difficulty. Comfortable accommodation and a ready cash flow cannot compensate for the loss of a parent, but lack of money and poor housing make a difficult situation even worse. Children of divorce have already been deprived of a parent. Material deprivation doubles the problem, and it is believed that poverty can put children at exceptional psychological risk.

Divorced parents also express a great deal of concern about the effect the divorce may have on the educational and emotional development of their children. Will they get behind with their work at school? Will they find it difficult to make friends because of their parents' broken relationship?

Opinions are divided. One set of statistics indicates that family break-up leads to lowered educational performance and psychological disturbance. Another comes to the conclusion that children from one-parent families do not differ significantly in their educational achievements, although they may have more emotional problems (ILEA survey 1968–9). Evidence from the British Medical Association suggests that children in one-parent families are emotionally healthy, and that overcoming their difficulties together can actually strengthen a family (facts from the Finer Report, vol. 2).

So who should divorced parents believe? Insecurity seems to be at the root of many problems. If the family is insecure financially, or the parent cannot cope with the emotional upheaval, the children will soon become anxious and start reflecting their distress in behaviour problems.

Sharing the burden
Some parents worry unnecessarily and create problems where none existed, but the fact that they no longer have a partner to share their worries can magnify them out of all proportion. Discussing the problems with people in a similar situation, or someone who can understand, helps to restore a sense of balance. It is also useful to remember that *all* children experience problems, especially during the troubled years of adolescence. It can be a great mistake to assume that the problem has arisen because of the divorce. Actually analysing where and why the trouble started may point to a different conclusion. Even if it does relate back to the divorce, parents would do well to remember that they themselves are not likely to have sailed through the proceedings without some element of emotional upset.

Allowing for the fact that the child is likely to take longer than the parents to realise the full implications of divorce proceedings should help parents not to expect too much, too soon. Because divorce is a bereavement experience for the children as well as the adult, they also need special allowances made while they come to terms with their grief.

Friends and relatives can play an important role in this healing process, providing they understand that both child and parent are going to need an extra amount of love and care. Grandparents are generally acknowledged to have a far greater reserve of patience than parents and can do a great deal to ease the situation when tensions and misunderstandings start to build up. Often an 'independent arbitrator' is needed to explain why the parent is reacting so aggressively, or to help the parent see that the child is only expressing anger and frustration similar to their own but with far less restraint!

Other adults can also provide the extra cuddles and affection that the children need, but their own parent is incapable of supplying at that particular point of time. Children who find a sympathetic adult may allow their hidden grief to come spilling out in the conversation – once they are away from the parents' presence and the fear of adding to their distress.

Trying to fulfil the role of father and mother is another headache for the single parent. Mothers worry about having to be 'too firm', fathers are concerned that their children lack a mother's love. It is generally agreed that children need both a male and female pattern in order to develop into balanced individuals. Does that mean children from one-parent families have less chance of developing normally? One lone father was worried because his son reacted unfavourably towards women. Then the boy started nursery school and was able to develop good relationships with the women staff. Mrs Dee was upset because her son was afraid of men. She mentioned the matter to the child's headteacher who went out of his way to send the boy on special errands for him.

Belonging to a group where there is a general feeling of fellowship and family can also provide models of the missing sex. Many lone parents hated the idea that their child was 'different' and appreciated it when the child was accepted and absorbed into a group. Something as simple as kissing an extra child goodnight when tucking in your own on a church houseparty may not mean much to the father performing the deed, but can mean the world to a lone mother – and the child.

Feeling the odd one out

Helping a single-parent family feel accepted calls for a great deal of sensitivity. Seeing another family functioning as a unit, complete with Mum and Dad, can bring home the pain of your own loss and some young mothers were only able to visit their friends when they knew the Dads would be at work, and their children would not need to feel the odd ones out.

Social occasions can be another time when lone parents and their children are vulnerable. One parent felt very self-conscious when she had to attend the parents' evening at her son's school. She was convinced she would be the only one without a partner. Weddings presented even more problems. Who gives the bride away if her father disappeared from the scene many years ago? Should one or both parents be invited to the wedding? If they both came, would they speak to one another? 'I would have thought my parents could have got over their differences by now,' said one bride, voicing the hurt of many others when she realised her wedding day would be marred by a conflict that had not been of her making.

Getting a balance

Although it is highly unlikely that any child can come through the pain and separation of divorce without scars, parents can be aware of possible danger points and take avoiding action. 'I had to be very careful not to use the boy to take his father's place,' said Barbara, 'nor to burden him with things that were worrying me but were obviously too grown-up for him.' That does not mean to say that children in a single-parent family are incapable of shouldering their fair share of household duties and responsibilities. Problems are only likely to come if they are given too much responsibility, or no responsibility whatsoever. Spoiling is poor compensation for the loss of a parent.

One lone parent described his position as a 'balancing

act'. It can be so easy to be over-possessive and take away the child's sense of independence, or to shrug off a child's attempt at affection when you are turned in on your own hurt. Children need freedom to be themselves, coupled with the security of a love that cares. An educational psychologist, writing in the summer 1976 issue of the journal for one-parent families, said children need 'a positive, creative love – not a smothering, possessive love.'

Only children are particularly 'at risk' because of the demands a lone parent may make upon them. One young wife whose father left home when she was still a child felt life had been a continual conflict to 'get away' from the mother. 'She's like something hanging over me – domineering,' she explained. 'She still treats me as if I was about nine. I only got married as early as I did to get away.'

Another kind of balancing act may be needed when the parents' interests and needs conflict with those of the children. What do you do if you have two young daughters at home on holiday when you are struggling to finish some decorating, or complete a piece of office work? 'I faced the situation squarely,' said their father. 'I just couldn't do as much work as I would have liked. I did the essentials then I spent the rest of the day with them.' Other times the parents' needs may have to take priority – just as they would in a two-parent family.

Personality clashes can also be a problem in a single-parent family for there is no third party to intervene. If the child resembles the absent partner it is not unknown for the remaining one to subconsciously take out their hidden aggression on the child. Parents aware of possible problem areas with their children could do worse than the father who knew he needed to be constantly 'on guard' in his relationship with his daughter – to admit his own inadequacies, as well as hers.

No parents are perfect and having sole responsibility for the growth and development of a child can be a frightening task. An Anglican minister on a large council estate is convinced that a parent bringing up children on their own should get support from other people in the congregation. Practical help such as baby-sitting or house maintenance is always appreciated, but lone parents may be even more in need of assistance with the involved problems of relationships, particularly with teenage children.

'I think our western view of the nuclear family has been too small,' the minister said. 'It seems to have isolated people and made them very lonely. Probably the biblical idea of a family is the extended family. There's more strength in its variety and size.' He sees the Church as an extended family sharing in God's work of caring for orphans, protecting widows, and giving 'the lonely a home to live in' (Ps. 68.5–6. GNB).

Sociologists would probably agree that many of the practical difficulties encountered by one-parent families could be minimised if the family group was not so fragmented, or if there were some substitute to replace it. The welfare state may have taken over many of the responsibilities, but the demands on the existing services are ever increasing. Social workers attempt to provide support for the single parent, but their time is limited and their case loads full. So who can a single parent turn to for help when things get on top of them, or the children seem to be getting out of hand?

Working with the school
If school work appears to be suffering the obvious person to consult is the child's teacher, or headteacher. They may be just as perplexed as the parent if a child's work or behaviour suddenly, or unaccountably, deteriorates, and be glad of a chat with the parent. All teachers study a limited amount of child psychology in their basic training and will usually make special allowances for a child under stress. They may also be able to reassure the parent that the setback should be only temporary.

In more extreme cases, where the child's work or behaviour suffers over a prolonged period, the headteacher may ask an educational psychologist to see the child in the hope that appropriate professional help may be suggested.

Finding it all too much
If the child is exhibiting no obvious signs of stress in their work and relationships at school but the parent is unable to cope at home, the doctor is the person to consult. He may suggest temporary palliatives such as tablets to take some of the immediate strain out of the situation, or refer the family to child guidance. Parents may resent the fact that when there are problems with children the professionals are likely to turn the spotlight back on them and their relationships, but a child's behaviour is frequently a mirror of the parents' attitudes or state of mind.

Parents can also refer a child direct to the child guidance clinic if the school or doctor does not think it necessary, but the parent does. Unfortunately, it may take a while to arrange an appointment with a professional adviser, and when a parent has reached screaming pitch the need of help is immediate. Where can a single parent turn if their own family live miles away, and they are marooned in a multi-storey block of flats, in imminent danger of venting their frustration on the children?

The NSPCC can be contacted for advice and help on their twenty-four-hour telephone service on 01-580-8812. Samaritans may also help to take the heat out of a tense situation. Their telephone number will be listed under 'S' in the telephone directory, or in the local newspaper.

Parents Anonymous is a relatively new, but growing group, working on similar lines to Samaritans. They try to maintain a twenty-four-hour service where parents under stress can ring for help (see address on page 129). Groups already exist in areas as far apart as Birmingham and Brighton, Sheffield and Southampton, and local groups will probably be advertised in regional newspapers. The emphasis is on parents helping other parents, by listening to their problems and by understanding and befriending them. Some areas operate day centres or support groups where parents meet to share their problems, or simply get away from them for a time. If expert advice is needed the volunteers can usually direct a caller to the appropriate agency.

Winning through

As in all families, there are bound to be difficulties but providing the parent is not left to struggle alone there is no reason why they should not be overcome. If family and friends rally round with practical help and support, the lone parent could well find that, 'The kids are fine. They're better adjusted and behaved than some whose parents are still together.'

The problems are more likely to come when one adult is left to shoulder all the responsibility, or is unable to handle their own hurt and make a new life for themselves and the children. Of course it will take time. Wounds do not heal overnight, particularly the deep psychological ones. But divorced parents have been delightfully surprised to find how resilient children can be, given continuing love and a sense of security.

One mother was staggered to hear her son describing 1973 as the happiest year of his life. He seemed to have completely forgotten that was the year his father left home! Yet that family had all suffered in the beginning. Their home in the country had been sold, they had to move back into an older house in the town, the children had to start at a new school, make new friends. Mother could only cope with the aid of tablets . . . but they had come through. 'We are a unit of three now,' she explained. 'We have quite a good little routine going.'

In fact children are often the main reason a parent manages to fight through. To know a child's happiness and well-being depended on their instinct to survive could be the very incentive needed to bring an adult through their depression and grief. 'The children were a tremendous strength,' said Barbara. 'I knew there was nobody else to look after them the way I wanted them to be looked after. Their father had gone and it was just as if the Lord was telling me, "Right. Stand up. Pull yourself together. You've got a job to do."'

Nobody would pretend bringing up children singlehanded is an easy task, but it can be done. There will be tears, there will be clashes of personality, but given perseverance and the ability to examine your own failings as well as the children's, a new and deeper relationship is possible. Sandra's husband walked out when she was three months' pregnant, leaving her to bear their son, and rear him and their eighteen-month-old daughter singlehanded.

'Me and my son are friends now,' she said. 'Mind you, my relationship with him had to be worked on and prayed a lot about. There were times when I hated him. He was so much like my husband. I didn't realise what I was doing at the time. I used to get in such a temper with him if he was naughty, but he wasn't really worse than any other child. It was just that my hate and anger were vented on him. He was a man and I blamed all men. I had to have a lot of prayer to be healed of the hurt I was feeling, but I also had to pray a lot for him, for the damage I'd done to him in how I'd treated him. It took years to develop our relationship and get us sorted out.'

But what an achievement to be able to say 'Me and my son are friends.' I wonder how many parents in a so-called 'normal' family could say that?

Questions for discussion or personal meditation

1. What special problems do single-parent families face? Should they be expected to cope alone? Who could share in the task? How?

2. a) Do you know the addresses of agencies in your area that help and support single-parent families, or families 'at risk'?

   b) What do you know of the work of –
   Gingerbread
   NCOPF
   NSPCC
   Parents Anonymous?

   c) Would you recommend a secular agency to someone in need of help? (Say why, or why not.)

3. What does your Church do to help and support families under stress? What could they do? What could you do?

12

Practical and financial problems

The home is the major source of capital in most families and reaching an agreement about how it should be shared after a divorce can be fraught with difficulty.

Some brave souls have attempted remaining in the same house as the divorced partner but that presents obvious difficulties, especially if children or a third party are involved. If the home has to be split the courts usually take a 'one-third starting point' as their basic principle, but even when the property is shared fifty-fifty there are bound to be disagreements. Watching a partner dividing the home, along the lines of 'That's yours, that's mine', can be incredibly painful.

So many emotions and vested interests are involved in the break-up of a home that various recommendations have been made for a 'conciliation service' to help partners reach a settlement as harmoniously as possible. At the moment the legal profession bears the brunt of this difficult job. Friends and relatives can thoughtlessly aggravate the situation by encouraging the partners in a one-sided view of their claims on the property and possessions.

The factors most likely to influence a child's ability to cope with divorce, next to the need for emotional stability, are in fact the arrangements made concerning housing and money. To lose a parent can be damaging. To lose a parent and the security of a familiar environment can be devastating. Where the children are going to live and what financial provision is being made for their upbringing are likely to be the first considerations of the judge when deciding who has care and custody.

A roof over your head

Because the whole business of home ownership is fraught with legalities it is important to seek advice as soon as possible even if the property is rented from the local council. (See list of helpful books and agencies on page 129) According to the National Council for One Parent Families, one-third of the people involved in divorce proceedings are faced with finding a new home, and women with children are particularly vulnerable if they leave the home. Those with tied homes, such as clergy and farm labourers, are also likely to find themselves in a difficult situation, with little capital and no prospect of having the tenancy transferred.

Setting up a new home on a fraction of the former capital also poses problems. Division of the property invariably means neither party has sufficient to purchase a home of comparable quality to the original. If there are children and the wife retains possession of the home, the arguments may continue until the house can be sold and divided perhaps when the children have ceased full-time education or reached the age of eighteen.

Wives may find they are fighting a losing battle to maintain a property single-handed. If it is Dad who has been deserted even the most determined may find running a home, looking after the children and holding down a regular job too much of a strain. One father could 'barely afford' domestic help, but got so depressed and over-tired he decided an extra pair of hands was an essential for his sake and the children's. Others find they have to give up a full-time job and exist on social security, rather than run the risk of having the children taken into care.

Maintenance

Claiming supplementary benefit may require swallowing a certain amount of pride and it may barely cover expenses if it *is* paid, but at least it is a regular source of income. The families in an unenviable position are the ones who are *supposed* to be paid maintenance which often fails to materialise. Apparently two and a half thousand men are imprisoned annually for not paying maintenance, and the whole issue is surrounded by controversy.

Younger, 'liberated' women may have no desire to be dependent on a man with whom they have no further legal or emotional ties. Women with children claim it is impossible to get a job with twelve weeks' annual holiday, and if they cannot work they must somehow be supported. Older women who have spent their lives rearing children and running a home may have no qualifications or training to fit them for work, even if age was not against them.

Men find maintenance an equally bitter pill to swallow. The man paying mortgage repayments for a house he can no longer occupy, plus maintenance for his wife and children, may find he has very little left in his pocket to cover his own expenses, even if officially he should have sufficient to maintain a 'reasonable standard of living'. When a second wife arrives on the scene the situation becomes even more complicated as the court can order maintenance *against* a husband, depending on the second wife's income and capital state. 'In my worst moments I look on maintenance as an imposition,' said one man who finds that the joint income of himself and his second wife is barely enough to cover essentials, once maintenance has been paid to his first wife and children.

During her speech at the second reading of the 1971 Matrimonial Property Act, Lady Summerskill maintained that 'most men cannot afford two wives'. Apart from those in the very high income bracket it seems she was right.

Money

Money, or rather the lack of it, is one of the major headaches for one-parent families. According to a survey in 1976 their average weekly income is half that of a two-parent family, and it is estimated that one-parent families are the fastest growing group at poverty level.

Statistics show that in November 1977 nearly a third of lone parents receiving supplementary benefit were divorced women with children.

Part of the problem with supplementary benefit is the myth that anyone on social security is a scrounger. Friends and relatives may react with horror when a divorcee admits they are going to apply for free school meals or supplementary benefit, little realising the conflict involved in making that decision. Far better the commonsense, supportive approach of Barbara's aunt. 'She *made* me go to social security,' Barbara said. 'I absolutely hated the thought – possibly because of pride, or fear, or a mixture of both. In the end she came with me and refused to leave until I'd seen someone. I think she knew that if she left I would have come out. I had to stand there and keep on saying to myself, "I'm not here for me. I'm here for the children."'

Like many others, Barbara was caught in a 'poverty trap' where it is impossible to work because of the children, and the low wages or long hours where employment is available. What about those who decide they must get out of the house regularly – if only to preserve their sanity?

Finding alternative care for young children when a lone parent is working is a very real problem. The break-up of family units means that relatives who might be willing to help rarely live close enough. Day nurseries run by a local authority are much in demand, but only 0.7 per cent of the pre-school population manage to obtain a place. Nursery schools and playgroups are of tremendous benefit to children but are mostly part-time. A number of parents leave their children with child-minders, but this can be expensive and they do not all fulfil the law's requirements. Some places of employment provide a crèche for children but they are few and far between.

It might be assumed that the situation would ease once children start school but there is still the worry of before and after school, holidays and sickness. Some local authorities organise play-centres, or help to coordinate voluntary activities during the longer school holidays, but this provision is still insufficient to meet the demand.

Sharing the burden

It has been suggested that friends and neighbours in the local community could do a great deal to help. Not everyone may be capable of caring for a pre-school child all day, every day, but they could maybe help out for a couple of hours after school while Mother does the shopping, or care for a child who is not desperately ill but not well enough to return to school. Offers to baby-sit occasionally can also be a real boon to a lone parent who is beginning to feel a social outcast.

Different patterns of need are bound to emerge in different areas but Church groups concerned about reaching and serving the local community would do well to study and assess the needs of single-parent families, to see how they can relieve some of the presssure on parents and children. If it is not feasible to organise anything on a large scale, there are still innumerable small ways in which the burden can be shared.

'People have been very good inviting us out to meals,' said Barbara. 'If you don't have to buy a Sunday joint that money can go towards some wallpaper or some clothes for the children. Holidays were out, until someone bought us the train tickets so that we could go and stay with a friend. My parents are a great help. They give the children clothes and a small game for their birthdays now, instead of just a big game, and they help with the children's pocket money.'

Maintaining the property is another area where assistance is usually appreciated. We may not be skilled in counselling, or able to assist financially, but single parents spoke with gratitude of the dad who wall-papered the living-room, the mum who showed them how to mend a fuse, and the neighbour who unblocked the drains.

Questions for discussion or personal meditation

1. Look around your home. How would you feel if it had to be split with somone else? What would you find most distressing?

2. How do you react to moving home? Remember the last time, *honestly*. Remember the delays, the insecurity, living out of packing cases, having to make new friends, finding your way round a new area. How might you feel if you had to do it with half the capital and no partner to share the frustrations? How could you help someone going through this experience?

3. Could you manage on half your present income?
   a) How would you react if you had no choice but to manage?
   b) What would you have to go without?
   c) How would you feel about that?
   d) How do you think your children would react?

4. Has your Church ever assessed the patterns of need in your area, such as what percentage of single parent families there are?
   a) Are they concentrated in any particular spot?
   b) Are there single-parent families in your street or block?
   c) What happens to the children before and after school, and during the holidays if the parent goes out to work?
   d) What provision is made for the parent who stays home all day, every day?

5. Has your Church considered other needs, such as unemployment, bad housing, high proportion of elderly, immigrant families with language problems, bored housewives, violence? What is your Church/ fellowship doing? What could they be doing?

6. Are you reaching out and serving the local community?

13

The divorcee in society

Sorting out the practical details of divorce is far from easy but coming to terms with the emotional and spiritual repercussions can be devastating. No matter how disturbed the marriage relationship has been, or how carefully people *thought* they had prepared themselves for the break-up, actually coping with a divorce is a different matter.

Change of status
For a start, there is the change of status. Many forms ask if a person is married or single. How do the newly-divorced phrase their reply, especially if they are embarrassingly aware of the queue of people waiting behind them as they fill in the form. They are no longer married, so presumably they should class themselves as single? Then how do they explain the two toddlers in the baby buggy, and the wedding ring glinting on their left hand? The number of people getting divorced may be rising annually but there is still a certain social stigma attached. Most people are reluctant to announce their new status to all and sundry, particularly if they have not had time to admit the situation to themselves. People spoke of feeling 'ashamed', or were uncertain how to describe themselves 'You've still got children, so you're really half married,' said a bewildered Barbara. 'But you're not a housewife any more. What are you? A housemother?'

Social gatherings
Living in a society where it is the norm to be married

(over ninety-five per cent of women and ninety-one per cent of men have been married by the age of 40 according to *Social Trends*, 1979) does not improve matters. People soon begin to feel outcasts if they are the only person by themselves at a social gathering. Whether it is a dinner party, an outing to the theatre or a dance makes little difference. Taking a friend can ease the problem, but many people tend to withdraw from social life. Where events, such as weddings, can not be avoided the sense of being 'out of the ordinary' can be particularly painful, especially if the divorced person has a prominent role and no escort. Family occasions also revive the sense of loss and isolation. Watching your sister and her husband with their children can be very distressing if *your* husband has left the family unit. 'The most harmless-looking things throw you,' explained Mrs Dee. 'Like a friend's husband coming in from work and greeting her with a kiss. You suddenly realise it won't happen to you again.'

Weekends

And what about the times families traditionally spend together? Weekends can be dreaded rather than greeted with delight if the partner has the children and you are left to face Saturday and Sunday alone. Even when the children are around, Sundays can become a nightmare. If the family had been used to going out with Dad, organising alternative occupations on a limited budget daunts all but the most resourceful. Yet if they remain indoors the day seems endless. 'I've never adjusted to being alone on a Sunday,' said one woman who had been divorced four years. 'But some friends invite us round alternate Sundays and that helps.'

People left completely on their own are particularly vulnerable at weekends and during holidays. If they go out they cannot escape the other couples and families enjoying themselves. If they stay in they face the prospect of their own company for hours, maybe days, on end. Some 'line up jobs' to help pass the time, others stick to a routine, such as cooking a Sunday lunch for 'something to do'. One person described walking to the opposite side of town to visit her sister – just to get out of the house and see someone, if only for a cup of tea and a quick chat. This is where friends can be of real assistance. They may not be able to entertain a divorced person for the whole weekend, but an invitation to Sunday lunch, or tea, or even just a cup of coffee can break the monotony of a weekend which must seem unending. Barbara's aunt invited her to stay if ever she felt low. She never actually went for more than Sunday lunch. Just to know there was somewhere she *could* go was sufficient.

Christmas

Normal holidays are difficult, but family festivals such as Christmas can be agony. The fact that there is no longer a partner to share the pleasure of opening presents can reduce the most hardy to tears. Children miss the absent parent; parents are conscious of their children being the only ones in the family gathering without a dad or mum.

Some parents did manage to overcome their differences sufficiently to spend at least an evening together sharing presents and greetings, if only 'for the sake of the children'. Others solved the problem by having two Christmases – one with each parent. Those on a limited income trying to budget for all the 'extras', or coping with a job plus the Christmas shopping and planning, could feel the whole 'season of goodwill' just too much to bear.

In fact any change in, or addition to, the normal routine can create problems. Moving home, changing employment, a bereavement or unexpected illness may prove an intolerable burden for someone whose resources are already stretched to the limit. Whether they cope with the crisis or 'go under' could depend almost entirely on the amount of support they receive from family and friends.

Attitude of society

Because of their aroused sensitivity, the way other people react to them can make or break a person grappling to come to terms with the demands of their new lifestyle. All of us are capable of asking the wrong question at the wrong moment. It is how we cope with our embarrassment that matters, whether we stammer in confusion, apologise profusely or turn the question into a genuine expression of concern. 'I can't stand people being embarrassed,' said Mike. 'That makes me embarrassed too.'

Distress is also caused if friends and neighbours expect too much, too soon. Someone who has recently experienced the trauma of divorce and the undermining of their faith and self-confidence is unlikely to be able to resume a leadership position immediately, or to act as a spiritual dynamo. Simply reading the Bible or praying may require a superhuman effort. If their feelings of inadequacy and guilt are reinforced by harsh judgements, or ostracism from Christian society and service, the divorced person may come to believe that God will no longer accept them either.

Sometimes old wounds can be opened by the unthinking assumption that everyone over the age of twenty-one should be married, or by expecting divorcees to react with delight to the latest escapades of a spouse they would rather forget. Mrs Dee still suffers when her ex-husband's misdeeds get splashed across the local paper, or the woman in the corner shop regales her with accounts of his various unsavoury acquaintances. 'I don't want to hear,' said Mrs Dee. 'I feel bitter in a way, because I haven't any happy memories, and therefore I don't want to be reminded.'

Memories and meetings

Unfortunately, because it is a small community she cannot avoid meeting him in the street. How does she cope with that? 'It brings it all back again,' she said. 'I don't feel strong enough to ignore him. When I get home I sit thinking about it and wondering why I had to meet the wretched man.'

The lucky ones may escape by moving to a different area, but those tied to the locality by a job, or housing, or the children's schooling find meeting the ex-spouse is a recurring irritation. Most people hope the legal ending of the marriage will mean the end of the relationship, but when the spouse lives locally or has regular access to the children that is not the case. For a start, the children may not accept that the relationship is broken and do all in their power to revive it. 'You can't stop their memories', said Barbara. 'They don't know the pain that went on behind their backs.'

The ones who coped most ably with unexpected meetings were the couples whose marriages had lasted a matter of months rather than years. Part of this could be attributed to lack of time to build up a relationship of any depth, but it may also be partly due to the adaptability of youth. Several of the under-twenty-fives spoke of regarding their former spouse 'as an old schoolfriend', or an 'acquaintance from the past'. But none of them had children. Their meetings were usually casual and short-lived, and most had work or new friendships to divert their attention.

Visiting a former home did cause distress however, especially if the second home did not bear comparison or a new partner had taken up residence. The thought of another person sharing the life of someone you have once loved is never easy to accept. Barbara felt very old at thirty-four when she realised her husband's new wife was only in her early twenties. Another woman reacted rather more violently to her husband's 'dolly bird' and feared she might express her fury if they met in the street.

Time is probably the greatest healer in this situation. One woman had been deeply hurt by her husband's obvious happiness with his second wife. She still loved him and had found the parting a great wrench. Now, six years later, she is able to view them as 'just another married couple' – much to her relief.

Physical relationships

The early days of separation were inevitably the hardest. Those who had experienced a satisfactory physical relationship found great difficulty in accepting that it should suddenly come to an end. But sexual frustration was only part of the picture. There was the loss of affection and security to contend with as well. 'You do become part of one another, intertwined,' said Barbara. 'When he left it was as though half of me had been torn away, and I missed having somebody to cuddle up to on a cold night.'

If a relationship had deteriorated to such an extent that the physical side had also been unsatisfactory people found less difficulty in adjusting. But sex is a powerful impulse and people reacted in a variety of ways to deprivation.

Some found their sense of trust had been so undermined by the breakdown of their marriage they had little confidence in the opposite sex, and tended to avoid them in case 'the same thing happened again'. This could lead to an unreasonable fear of being near, or even speaking to, the opposite sex. At the other extreme, people attempted to substitute for the lost relationship in an excess of alcohol or pornography – until they realised those things created as many problems as they solved.

Those whose partners leave them in favour of somebody else may find their sexual instincts actually heightened, and the resulting dreams and fantasies difficult to cope with. In such circumstances it is not uncommon for men and women to masturbate, although many despise themselves for doing so. What advice would a qualified counsellor give to those experiencing such feelings of guilt and frustration? 'To look upon it as an unhappy substitute if it makes life more bearable,' said Alison. 'And to console themselves with the thought that they will not always find it necessary.'

Women suddenly deprived of a partner often find consolation in taking their children into their bed. Is this another cause for anxiety? Alison thinks not and believes it is more for the comfort of having another body nearby than for any hidden sexual motivation, though there could be problems if the practice continued for any length of time. Holding a friend's hand, or greeting them with a hug or kiss may raise a few eyebrows, but could mean all the difference to someone desperately in need of reassurance and love. Of course there are dangers, but if people are aware of them it is possible to take avoiding action. Clergy and their wives may find particular problems in coming to terms with the fact that the minister can easily become the focus of the fantasies and affection of women whose husbands have left them. 'We cope with this by Colin acting as their vicar, and me becoming their friend,' said Alison.

If the Church community side-steps the issue and people do not receive the affection they need, the temptations are obvious. One reaction is to rebound into a new relationship, or series of relationships. In the short term this appears to be therapeutic – if people are reassured they are still attractive. But complications can arise with divorce proceedings, and further hurt be experienced when one or other backs out. Sometimes the new partner is not willing to enter a long-term relationship that could involve shortage of money, and coping with someone else's children. At other times the threat of being cited as co-respondent in divorce proceedings frightens them off.

Another factor to be considered is the effect a parent's relationship can have upon the children. It would be unrealistic to suggest that parents should forfeit all friendship but they need to be aware of the distress and insecurity created by friendships which do not last. 'Be discreet,' warned a consultant psychologist.

Divorced people do tend to balk at anything which might involve a new commitment. They want a stable relationship, then hesitate or back out for fear it might not work. In such situations everyone is a loser. A chain of hurt, bewildered people are left in their wake, and a sense of inadequacy and guilt is compounded with each failed relationship. Jeff was brutally honest about this predicament. 'I am very lonely and consequently very vulnerable,' he said. 'I need sex and I need a woman, but I have in effect been using women. I tend to fall in love, or imagine myself in love, but I don't know if I love anybody enough to marry them. It's wonderful to be loved, but then I begin to feel restricted. I'm really torn up about this.'

Guilt is a common feature of such brief relationships; guilt about hurting yet another person, guilt about offending against previously accepted moral codes, plus a revival of all the feelings of failure associated with the break-up of the original marriage.

The most balanced attitudes came from those who had faced up to the situation, admitted their need but realised there was more to life than a hunger for sex. They might experience pangs of regret occasionally but they quickly occupied their minds (and bodies) with other things, or joked themselves out of it.

A young clergyman whose wife had left him was confronted with a dilemma. His bishop asked if he had any sexual problems. When he replied, 'No, father,' the bishop remarked drily, 'You're jolly lucky. Most of us' do.' The clergyman knew then that he had fallen into a trap and that his bishop would not be satisfied with anything less than an honest answer. He had to face the subject realistically. 'What do you suggest I do?' he asked. 'I don't have a wife and the church frowns upon re-marriage. I can either resort to a prostitute, or have an affair – neither of which you would approve. And as I regard sex as an integral part of love neither of them appeals to me.' He concluded there was very little he could do about it – other than accept the situation.

Loneliness
In fact, he refuses to believe that re-marriage is out of the question even if it would mean leaving the priesthood. But the loss of a sexual partner is only part of the problem. The Anglican prayer-book describes marriage as being for 'the mutual society, help, and comfort, that

the one ought to have of the other' and however
tenuous the marriage relationship might be, adjusting
to life without a companion is not easy. Men grieve the
loss of their children, women miss their husbands
coming home from work every night.

Even the television blaring in the corner cannot
dispel the fears and tensions that night-time brings.
Why does the dog keep barking? Is someone snooping
around outside, or is it simply a neighbour's cat on the
prowl? What happens if you are taken ill and nobody
knows? What about the future – ten, twenty years'
time? Does divorce commit you to a lifetime of loneliness? Mrs Dee has been separated from her husband for
ten years but she still finds loneliness a terrible thing.

'You can be with a crowd and still be alone,' she said.
'I've been at home with aunts, uncles, my Mum and
Dad, all the children, and I've been crying inwardly,
even though I've laughed and acted the fool with them.
If I go to bed with a little problem it grows into a moun-
tain in the night. If there's nobody to share it with, you
worry about the silliest things. Then you start feeling
sorry for yourself and end up with a fit of depression.'

She manages to cope – with the support of her friends
and family, and a bottle of tranquillisers. But the battle
has not been easy, and victory is far from certain. There
are days when she still wonders if it is worth the effort.
People concerned about the effects of divorce on their
friends and relatives can do much to help so that they do
not give up the struggle.

Questions for discussion or personal meditation

1. Have you ever felt the odd one out? How did you
cope with your sense of isolation? What advice and/or
practical help could you give to someone experiencing a
similar sensation?

2. When do people on their own feel most vulnerable?
If the Church is an extended family, and many of our
festivals are 'family' occasions, should their loneliness
be a rebuke to us? What can we do about it?

3. Consider the problems someone deprived of a partner can experience.
   a) What part can the Church family play in re-assuring them and loving them?
   b) What are the inherent dangers if this task is left to one person?
   c) What safeguards need to be employed?
4. Why do we find sex so difficult to discuss? What would you say to someone experiencing sexual frustration following bereavement or divorce?
5. What can divorcees do to help themselves?

14

Survival

In the early days of the marriage breakdown when the individual is suffering the worst effects of numbness or shock, anything or anyone who will shoulder the burden of day-to-day living is welcome. This is when a number of people instinctively turned to God. Barbara prayed the same prayer every night for several months, 'God give me strength to cope with tomorrow,' and discovered that he did. Others found new hope and acceptance in the Christian family. 'You're open to anything when you're on your own,' said Sandra. 'I tried alcohol and ouija, besides trying to commit suicide. If I hadn't found God I don't know where I'd be – in the middle of a breakdown, or up in the West End in a strip club, I expect.'

Being accepted by other people is a vital part of the healing and rebuilding process, and can mean the difference between a person having strength to go on and grapple with their problems, or giving up in despair. Sandra found new hope when a friend shared her hurt by praying, and crying, with her regularly. Jeff is fighting a continuing battle over the custody of his children, and also with his own soul. He reckons he can almost feel the forces of good and evil struggling for ownership, and acknowledges that he desperately needs the support of friends who will love and accept him without judgement when he launches into another romance or bout of drinking.

Need of friendship
But where do people find the love and friendship they

need? High-rise flats, impersonal estates, television, noisy machinery, and the break-up of the family unit have all played their part in destroying relationships. A minister's wife on a council estate with a large proportion of broken homes, sees a vital part of their Church's ministry as organising social events where lonely people can make new friends and find they are accepted as part of the fellowship. Others find practical help and emotional support through groups like Gingerbread, or friends who are happy for them to 'drop in' during the lonely hours when the children are at school, or who drag them out for an evening regardless of their protests.

People suffering a sense of betrayal after a broken marriage rarely feel like exposing their hurt to the glare of a large-scale social gathering, but do appreciate being taken out, or sharing a meal with a small group of close friends. A visit to the theatre, or a small private party may also help to establish some feeling of normality, providing they are fully integrated into the group and not left to feel an 'outsider'. Going out with someone in a similar situation, or simply chatting over their fears and frustrations is another safety valve.

Mrs Dee finds her next-door neighbour is sympathetic without being soppy. 'She can calm me as quickly as anything,' she explained. 'I can go in there feeling dreadful and come out laughing. She's a true friend. I could talk to her about anything.' This is a complete contrast to the so-called 'fellowship' group at her Church. When she asked if they could spend an evening discussing divorce the reaction was anything but favourable. Mrs Dee consoled herself with the thought that as they were *strangers* they wouldn't understand anyway!

Need to be occupied
But even people with a reliable circle of friends find there comes a time when they can no longer spend the whole day depending on other people. Reality has to be faced eventually, and some form of routine established.

Children still have to be fed, clothes washed, beds made, and dogs taken for walks. Friends and family may be able to assume responsibility temporarily, but most have other commitments to claim their time and attention. Even if this were not so, it is not always a good thing to allow someone to take over your life completely, no matter how well-intentioned they may be.

Those who had sunk into lethargy at the beginning found the only way they could break out of it was by forcing themselves to do things until they got into a routine. Having a home to look after, or children to rear was an obvious incentive, so long as people made allowances for the effects of divorce, and didn't expect too much of them or their resources. Going out to work also helped 'to keep your mind off things', and gave people an outside interest. But working long hours on top of trying to run a home and family could be counter-productive.

Another hazard some people discovered was that of becoming obsessive – particularly if they lived alone. 'You are so used to doing things your own way you reach the point where you don't think anybody should upset your plans,' explained Mike. 'I even find myself getting irritated if someone puts the teapot back in the cupboard the wrong way.'

New independence
Getting things into perspective is more than half the answer. The instinctive reaction to rats under the floorboards, or a burst water-main is panic, and a frantic shout for husband. When husband is no longer available many women have been surprised and delighted to find that they can cope – with a little practice and perseverance. Decorating, gardening, fixing a curtain rail and changing a plug soon become part of daily routine, as does washing, cooking, and vacuuming for the men. What women's lib. groups have been campaigning for over several years may be achieved in a matter of weeks when divorce makes 'do-it-yourself' a necessity, rather than an added option.

New incentive

Coming to terms with the emotional repercussions unfortunately takes considerably longer. Those who find
difficulty in accepting that the marriage really has
broken take longest of all to adjust. Mike made repeated attempts at reconciliation. He just didn't believe
the marriage could be shattered after such a short time.
It wasn't until he met his wife's new boy friend on the
doorstep that he was brought up with a shock. From
then on, he took a more realistic attitude and decided to
build a new life, without excluding the possibility that
she might return. Once that decision had been made
other things began to slot into place. Work became
more interesting, his spiritual conflict decreased, and he
began to undertake new projects.

Another factor which helps people adjust to the situation is determination, or 'cussedness', as Jeff described
it. Sometimes wounded pride was at the root of it, sometimes the sheer instinct for survival. *I will survive* was
the title of a 1979 hit tune. Many divorced people would
grit their teeth and nod agreement.

New self-realisation

But building a new life is often preceded by a painful
period of demolition and self-examination. The feelings
engendered by divorce are not always those society
smiles upon. Jeff felt he would like to take his ex-wife
apart 'limb from limb' when she snatched the children
out of his custody. Later he read that the reason God
says, 'Vengeance is mine, I will repay' (Rom. 12.19), is
that humans aren't big enough to handle it. Jeff knew it
was true. He had looked into his own heart and discovered a potential murderer, rather than the 'good
guy' he formerly believed himself to be.

Others realised when it was too late that their own
inadequacies could well have contributed to the failure
of their marriage. 'If I'd learnt to accept myself before I
was married I might not have chosen the person I did, or
used her as an emotional crutch against the terror of the

111

world,' said one man regretfully.

Probably the people hardest hit by this new self-realisation are the ones who have never faced up to the frailty of their own humanity. 'How do you witness to people about how great and wonderful being a Christian is when you have a marriage in tatters?' Mike grieved. Fortunately he had the sense to go to his Bible and realise that it is full of characters who, for all their greatness, constantly fell short of God's standards. When a vicar friend confided that he was a neurotic-depressive obsessed by his failings, Mike decided he was not unique and that there might be a small part for him in God's kingdom after all.

New maturity

Facing up to unpleasant facts about yourself and your situation can lead to a new maturity. Divorce may be devastating at the time, but some were able to look back afterwards and see that good had come out of it. Andrew's life appeared to be in ruins – no wife, no job, no home, virtually ex-communicated by the Church fellowship. But he felt that through the experience God had been beckoning him on, teaching him to grow up.

'You don't teach a child to walk by always holding his hand,' he explained. 'You've got to step back sometimes and let it stumble towards you. I think that as we progress God takes a few more steps back and makes us reach up more. It's as if you have a hill in front of you and the more you get up it the more you're encouraged to get up the next bit. I still have a few little slips down, but never to the depths I plumbed at the beginning. Eventually you begin to realise you are maturing, becoming more of a whole person.'

Someone suffering the agony of a recent broken relationship may feel they will never scramble out of the mire of despair, but the majority of divorced people agreed that it does become 'easier over the years'. The details of the break-up begin to blur, and time does heal, even though the scars remain.

New identity and spheres of service

Divorce may undermine the individual's confidence in himself, but once he begins to realise it is possible to make a new life there are certain compensations. Thinking for yourself, planning your own future, doing what you like rather than what your partner thinks you ought to do, all help to create a new sense of self-esteem. Some people find themselves heading in completely new directions – applying for another job, enrolling for a degree course, taking on voluntary work, joining a club.

Because divorce is such a traumatic event, a number of those who have survived the experience share a desire to help others going through similar torment. Some are able to assist friends and neighbours who come to them when their marriage starts to crumble. Others find themsleves counselling with a new depth of understanding. Colin and Alison did not reach the divorce courts but one of the factors that propelled them into marriage guidance counselling was thanksgiving that their marriage had survived a particularly sticky patch. Jeff initially joined Gingerbread for help and support, but found his role changing over the weeks. As he became stronger and more stable he was able to encourage others.

Whatever their function – whether official or unofficial – the counsel given by those who have experienced marital upheaval is firmly based in reality, although not necessarily quite what people expect. In his new role of social worker, Andrew meets many couples whose marriages are in danger of breaking up. Andrew sympathises with their problems, but leaves them in no doubt that abandoning their partner is not the only option. His own marriage may not have worked but he knows from harsh experience that the alternative is not to be lightly undertaken.

Questions for discussion or personal meditation

1. If divorced people are 'open to anything', what challenge should that present to concerned Christians?

2. What is 'fellowship'? Is your fellowship group a meeting of strangers, or caring people 'bearing one another's burdens.'? Would someone deeply hurt by a recent experience be able to unwind and find support there? (Say why, or why not.)

3. Does time heal? What factors might indicate that someone was beginning to emerge from the tunnel?

4. How can a painful experience like divorce possibly 'work for good'?

15

To re-marry or not

With all the emotional, social and material problems
caused by divorce, it might be supposed that those who
have been through it no longer have any faith in marriage. On the contrary, they described it as a 'good insti-
tution', 'old-fashioned but still important', 'a
tremendous relationship'.

As in most areas of life, we learn from our mistakes
and the breakdown of a marriage can be a bitter lesson
for all involved. 'I felt it wasn't marriage that my
husband was against,' said Barbara, 'just me.'

Statistics are one measure of this continuing confidence in marriage for, according to the 1977 OPCS
survey, one in three marriages is now a re-marriage for
one or both partners. Didn't experience cause them to
hesitate before plunging into another relationship?
Surely the hurt and upheaval of divorce left people
afraid and suspicious?

Hesitancy
In the early days after the marriage break-up many did
express doubt about re-marriage. The hurt and upheaval of divorce did leave people suspicious and afraid.
Some had discovered the hard way that marriage demanded more than they were prepared to give. They
did not want to repeat the experience in a hurry.
'Having to adjust to someone else ... letting them
become part of you ... knowing everything about you
...' required too much of an effort. Others felt
betrayed by their partners and were afraid that 'it might
happen again'.

Once over the initial shock the majority of people were not averse to the idea of a new relationship sometime in the future but expressed fear that loneliness might push them into another disastrous experience.

On the rebound

'I could have gone into another relationship quite easily – just for the sake of having someone to go to bed with,' Sandra admitted. Fortunately caution warned her that she might be repeating the same mistakes she had made in her first marriage – a trap a number of people fall into. Statistics show that those who re-marry quickly often marry someone similar to the first partner. It is not until after the ceremony they begin to realise their mistake. Some, like Jeff, vacillated between their needs and their fears. They wanted stability and security but could never commit themselves when it came to the crunch.

Another temptation is to rebound into a relationship for the sake of a shoulder to cry on, for reassurance. If the friendship is allowed to grow naturally it may well develop into something more permanent but the danger in today's sex-orientated society is that people commit themselves to a physical relationship without realising the emotional and practical repercussions. 'You've got to have your eyes open,' Sandra advised. 'If you've had one hurt, it makes you aware that love isn't all roses. Don't be completely suspicious, but be careful.'

Be careful. Make sure. Be a hundred per cent convinced. The warnings came loud and clear. Divorce not only made people aware of basic inadequacies in their own character but made them question the motivation of others. Is this man really in love with me or does he regard me as a proposition? He lives in a council house. I have a home of my own. Does he think he can move in rent free?

Those who found most difficulty in adjusting to the idea of sharing their lives were the ones who had been on their own for some time and had coped quite capably, despite the odd patches of loneliness. Sandra was tormented by doubt right up till the wedding. Her first husband had bullied and moulded her into what he wanted. She had enjoyed the freedom divorce had given her. Would she find history repeating itself once she committed herself to another man? Would she be able to cope with having another person around the house after being on her own for several years?

If a disastrous first marriage had made someone painfully aware that the 'balance between dependence and independence is a difficult one to achieve', the prospect of a second marriage had to be carefully thought out.

Facing up to self
Modern divorce law has attempted to remove the concept of 'guilt' and 'innocence' except in extreme cases. Admitting that your own inadequacies and failings have contributed to the marriage breakdown must raise all kinds of questions about what chance of success the new relationship has.

'We might learn from the past, but our personalities remain largely unchanged and we are liable to make the same mistakes through the same weaknesses,' said Andrew. When he began to consider re-marriage he knew that his prospective wife must be made to see him as he really was. Marriage had forced him to realise that he was a 'combination of two quite incompatible traits'. He was a loner, but at the same time he was desperately dependent, and frequently conscious of loneliness. Would his new wife be hurt by his need to shut himself off from the rest of the world, especially if it coincided with a time when she needed his support? Could they each retain their own identity but at the same time be completely open to the needs and identity of the other? Andrew claims that asking yourself such searching questions is not being morbidly introspective, but by knowing your strengths and weaknesses you are more prepared to cope with possible areas of difference.

Coping with the emotional hang-ups is only one problem facing someone contemplating re-marriage. Divorce may terminate the legal contract but that is not necessarily the end of all contact with the former spouse. 'When my ex first knew I was going out with a chap he threatened to hit him,' said Sandra. Yet their marriage had been terminated for several years.

If the first marriage had not been officially terminated the new relationship was likely to face all kinds of complications, and threats. A couple might want to marry but feel they were walking a minefield in negotiations with the first spouse concerning divorce. The marriage may well have broken down irretrievably before the third person appeared on the scene, but any hint of a second marriage was likely to create an adverse response. If the third party was involved in the marriage break-up the atmosphere could be even more fraught. 'Why should I free him to marry *her*?' is a common reaction. It is not surprising that when they realise all the implications, a number of people are reluctant to proceed with a friendship if a divorce is pending, particularly if they stand in danger of being named as co-respondent in an adultery case.

Considering the children
If children are involved there is a special need to tread cautiously. It is one thing to feel certain about a prospective husband. The thought of taking on his children can be more daunting.

'I knew I was becoming attracted to Richard,' said Rita, 'but not to his children. I didn't like the idea of getting involved. I had enough with my own two without taking on two more. I gave it a lot of prayer and thought. It took me a long time to know in my mind whether it was right. You've got to think about whether the children will accept you for a start... and accept one another. If they don't you've got problems.'

Even with only one set of children there are still bound to be problems. Folklore abounds with stories of wicked step-parents, so children's subconscious fears can be magnified out of all proportion unless they receive reassurance and sympathetic understanding. False expectations can be equally damaging and need to be dealt with just as carefully. 'Richard spoke to his children about me before I came. He told them it wouldn't be easy,' said Rita. 'They would still be expected to help in the home. I wouldn't be a servant.'

In her useful book *The challenge of second marriage*, Angela Reed advises: 'Those considering second marriage would be well advised to weigh up all the pros and cons very carefully and try to understand fully everything that may be involved in becoming a step-parent. This is not a question of being cool and calculating but of acting responsibly in a matter which could affect several lives.'

Any such input of practical advice is to be welcomed for, although re-marriage is increasing, step-parents receive little or no guidance. Being a parent is difficult enough, coping with someone else's children raises all kinds of questions. Will the child accept you? Will you accept the child? How do you prepare two sub-teens for the presence of a father figure, a disciplinarian, after three years with no man about the house? How does a confirmed bachelor adjust to sharing his life and home with a wife and her two children? How will the woman cope as intermediary?

No child really wishes to be separated from a parent, and when a substitute arrives on the scene they are not likely to be welcomed over-enthusiastically. Where the children still have a good relationship with the natural parent it is difficult for the step-parent not to feel jealous, particularly if he cannot afford the 'lavish presents' and treats the real parent is supplying in an effort to maintain, or repair, the relationship. It must take a considerable amount of maturity and self-control to realise just how important it may be for the child to continue to have some form of contact with the parent.

Single people coming in as step-parents experience special difficulty. At least those who have been separated from their own children by divorce appreciate the conflicts and heartache of an absent parent and have no illusions about the joys, and horrors, of raising children. 'There are always under-the-surface problems,' one stepfather explained. 'It's no good avoiding them. You have to admit that there's going to be conflict.'

Telling the family
Broaching the subject of re-marriage to family and friends can also generate a fair amount of tension. Most parents worry about their 'children' – no matter how old they may be – and are reluctant to see them exposing themselves to further possible hurt. Many expressed horror or shock, especially if it was a case of a single person marrying a divorcee with children. Did they know what they were doing? Were they acting out of misplaced kindness? Could they cope with the responsibility of someone else's children? The questions came thick and fast.

Understandably most concern was expressed if it was felt that a person was rushing into a relationship, without giving due consideration to all the implications. On large housing estates unusual relationships could well be the norm, and accepted with a shrug of the shoulders. In small closed communities there was often unpleasant gossip and speculation. However thick-skinned they may pretend to be, few people are immune to harsh words, unkind criticism or malicious gossip, and far from achieving the desired effect too blatant opposition may drive a person into a defensive position. Because so much is at stake in a re-marriage people do need wise counsel and an honest opinion, even if they do not accept it.

Conflict and confusion
Barry had been a leader in his Bible-based Church for many years. When he realised he was falling in love with a divorced woman his mind was in a turmoil. It seemed as if God had brought them together and blessed their relationship, but would they be going against his will if they should marry? Barry prayed. He asked his minister for advice. He discussed his dilemma with Christian friends. He read and re-read the relevant passages in the Bible and prayer-book. 'Those whom God has

joined together let no man put asunder,' The instruction seemed clear enough.

But Barbara and her husband were divorced. He had married another woman. Furthermore, since her divorce Barbara had become a Christian. Barry believed that in Jesus she was a new creation. After much heart searching he concluded that because we have a God who can forgive it would not be outside his will if he helped provide a secure, Christ-centred home for Barbara and her children.

From his theological training Andrew knew that the teaching of Paul the apostle seemed to reinforce the idea that a divorced person should remain single. Andrew had already made himself unpopular in the Christian community by divorcing his wife. If he married another he could well be regarded as completely beyond the pale. Yet a new and beautiful relationship was developing, which surpassed even his wildest dreams. Could a caring God dangle before him a vision of beauty and fulfilment as a very real possibility only to snatch it away again, saying in effect, 'Sorry chum. You must now suffer the consequences of your folly for the rest of your life.' He had already suffered considerably, and knew that the scars would be permanent. If God was his Father and still loved him, would he condemn him to celibacy for the rest of his life? He came to two controversial conclusions. First that Jesus linked divorce and re-marriage in such a way that the divorcing of one *in order to* marry another was most reprehensible. There had been deep-rooted problems in his marriage, but that was not one of them. The marriage had well and truly 'broken down' before the new relationship developed.

But scripture teaches that sexual union binds a couple as if they were 'one flesh'. Did that mean he would be violating God's commands by forming a new relationship? Were two unions against God's specific design? According to Paul, widowers are allowed to re-marry, and he felt death was an appropriate analogy for a broken marriage. He decided he could classify himself along with the widowers and unmarrieds whom Paul advised, 'If you cannot restrain your desires, go ahead and marry – it is better to marry than to burn with passion.' (1 Cor. 7.9, GNB.)

It is possible to accuse Barry and Andrew of casuistry, of twisting theology to suit their own ends. But like Jacob, they had to wrestle with their conscience and their God in an effort to seek some solution to a dilemma which confounds archbishops, let alone the ordinary priest or layman.

Marriage is indissoluble, therefore there can be no remarriage, insist one group of scholars. If scripture allows divorce it seems to permit the right to re-marry, runs the counter-argument. It is not re-marriage that is the sin, but divorce. The controversy centres round verses such as Luke 16.18 where Jesus is quoted as saying, 'Every one who divorces his wife and marries another commits adultery, and he who marries a woman divorced from her husband commits adultery.' Does this teaching forbid re-marriage entirely, or by acknowledging divorce as possible (though not ideal) does it also allow for the possibility of remarriage?

The 1978 Lichfield Report hit the headlines when it recommended that divorcees should be allowed to remarry in church, but the Synod (or Parliament) of the Church of England was almost equally divided on the subject. Pastors, theologians, and the correspondence columns of the secular and religious press reflect this diversity of opinion. The pastoral implications are obvious.

If a clergyman believes that marriage should be permanent and exclusive, how does he deal with a couple who come asking God's blessing on a second relationship? How can he reconcile the high ideals of Christian marriage and the needs of those who have failed once, but are keen to make a new beginning?

Church discipline

Officially, the Catholic Church will not accept a civil divorce and will only agree to a service of re-marriage if the first marriage has been annulled. Unofficially, many parish priests appreciate the problems this can create and do all they can to assure parishioners they are not beyond the scope of God's love. The Free Churches have no overall policy. Any decision about re-marriage is left to the discretion of the minister and/or the local Church. This can mean that the Church will refuse to re-marry, or that services of re-marriage outnumber first marriages, depending on the policy and theology of the local Church.

At the moment, the Anglican Church exercises the strictest discipline. Although an Anglican priest may officiate at a service of re-marriage according to the law of the land, Church law does not permit the use of the marriage service to anyone who has a former partner still living. Nevertheless, some priests defy their bishop and in 1975 five hundred services did take place. Some clergy have got round the situation by performing a service of blessing after a civil marriage but the Lichfield Report recommended that the present use of such services should be brought to an end because of the risk of confusion between the service of blessing and the marriage service, as well as the 'fear that the church would be giving the impression that it had begun to marry all comers.' (*Marriage and the Church's Task*, p. 84.)

Clergy who perform a service of blessing admit that the situation is ridiculous. The Bishop of Chelmsford summarised their dilemma in the diocesan magazine in September 1978. 'This is logically and theologically absurd,' he wrote. 'But it is an absurdity that arises out of compassion and many find comfort in it as they start a new venture in marriage.'

Until the Church comes to a specific decision about re-marriage the discrepancies will remain, with one parish allowing services of dedication almost indistinguishable from the marriage service, another reluctantly agreeing to a simple ceremony, and a third refusing any kind of church service. The Lichfield Report has recommended that the Church of England should allow the marriage of divorced people in church, providing they can satisfy a pastoral inquiry of their good intent for the new marriage and express penitence for past faults. But what criteria do you use to discern who may or may not be married in church? How do you justify those decisions? How do you minister and finance such a system? Should penitence be expressed publicly or privately?

Second best

Given the confusion and controversy surrounding the subject, it is hardly surprising that 'the continuing trend towards more civil marriages is due entirely to the rising proportion of marriages involving divorced people.' (OPCS monitor-Marriages 1977.)

Some make that decision completely voluntarily, even if a civil service is seen as second best. 'We talked and prayed about it, and felt it was right to get married in a registry office,' said Barbara. 'There's no getting away from it. I had made my vows once and although it wasn't my fault the marriage had broken, obviously there were faults on both sides. So even if I could have got married in church I don't think I'd have wanted to.'

Some would dearly love a church wedding, but are hesitant to put themselves in a position where they could be rejected a second time, 'I was so hurt I would not consider the possibility of being hurt any more by going to churches who would refuse to marry us,' a former Free Church elder explained. 'We got married in a registry office.'

The biggest reservations came from those who had become Christians fairly recently and could not understand why they were not allowed to share their new-found happiness with the Church family and with God. 'The registry office isn't the same as the church service,' said Thelma. 'You don't feel God knows or cares when you're in a registry office, yet we felt it was his intention we should be together. So it was important that we had a blessing in the church afterwards. We didn't have any hymns or anything. The vicar read part of the service and then we had a prayer. It was very quiet – only five or ten minutes.'

Few people would dispute the need for some form of discipline but there is a world of difference between the discipline of a harsh, unyielding judge, and that of a caring, compassionate father. Pray God we get the balance right soon, for the sake of all who need our love and understanding. Marriage is under threat, and increasing concern is being expressed about the number of *second* marriage breakdowns. So many factors militate against its success; not least the backlog of problems that can be carried over from the first marriage.

Since interviewing people for this book, I can rarely sing the lines, 'Past put behind us – for the future take us', without grieving for all those who find divorce, and the effects of divorce, very difficult indeed to put behind them. We may not like it but marriages are breaking down.

'I don't approve of cancer,' said Colin, 'or of people dying young, but it's my job to be there, to be involved.' I wonder if we dare be involved? The opportunities are endless. The need immense. If those experiencing problems before, during, or after a marriage are to see any light at the end of the tunnel we all have a responsibility, not only to appreciate the difficulties but to do something about them – now.

Questions for discussion or personal meditation

1. What practical issues need to be considered before re-marriage? Why is it necessary to react with wisdom and sensitivity if someone asks for advice about re-marriage? Does this preclude discussing possible problem areas?

2. It has been suggested that those dealing with requests for re-marriage should not probe for innocence or guilt but should seek to see repentance over past failure, an attempt to overcome the problems which led to divorce, acceptance of counselling, and a good possibility of success for the new marriage. Do you agree?

125

(Say why, or why not.)

3. Is re-marriage possible for a Christian? (Say why, or why not.) Should re-marriage services be allowed in church . . .

    a) for all comers, b) not at all, c) in some circumstances?

4. How would you respond to someone acknowledging their need of prayer and support over problems in a re-marriage?

    a) Would you have any appreciation of the extra pressures facing someone in a second marriage – such as limited finance, coping with stepchildren, painful memories, grief and hurt that may not have been adequately worked through?

    b) Could you help them discover some positive way forward for the future?

    c) Dare you be involved?

Agencies and Organisations
which can help

1. **Marriage guidance and support**
   National Marriage Guidance Council –
   (Look in telephone directory under 'M' for Marriage. Select nearest centre. Ring for an appointment.)
   Institute of Marital Studies, Tavistock Centre, Belsize Lane, London, NW3 Telephone: 01–435–7111
   (Counselling for married couples, inquire about costs.)
   Catholic Marriage Advisory Council, 15 Lansdowne Road, London, W11 Telephone: 01–727–0141
   London Centre, 33 Willow Place, London, SW1 Telephone: 01–828–8307
   Church Army, St. Margaret's Vestry, Lothbury, London, EC2 Telephone: 01–606–8330 (counselling service).
   Highgate Counselling Centre, Tetherdown Halls, Tetherdown, Muswell Hill, London, N10 Telephone: 01–883–5427 (Help with personal problems).
   Westminster Pastoral Foundation, 23 Kensington Square, London, W8 5HN Telephone: 01–937–6956 (counselling and training centre).
   Alcoholics Anonymous, Box 514, 11 Redcliffe Gardens, London SW1 9BG Telephone: 01–352–9779 (ring or write for address of local counselling centre).
   Al-Anon Family Groups (for the families of alcoholics), 61 Great Dover Street, London, SE1 Telephone: 01–403–0888
   National Council on Alcoholism, 3 Grosvenor Crescent, London SW1 Telephone: 01–235–4182
   National Association for Mental Health (Mind), 22 Harley Street, London, W1 Telephone: 01–637–0741
   Gamblers Anonymous, 17/23 Blantyre Street, London, SW10 Telephone: 01–352–3060
   Family Planning Association, 27 Mortimer Street,

London, W1N 7RJ Telephone: 01–636–7866 (all inquiries about local clinics, etc).

Family Network, National Children's Home HQ, 85 Highbury Park, London, N5 1UD. Telephone: 01–226–2033 (Telephone or 'pop in' service. Needs volunteers. Centres being organised in several parts of England, Wales and Scotland. Puts people in touch with experts dealing in family problems.)

National Women's Aid Federation, 374 Grays Inn Road, London, WC1 Telephone: 01–837–9316 or 837–3762 (Supporting agency for mentally and physically battered wives – and their children – gives legal, financial and housing information, talks over problems, puts women in touch with local refuges throughout the country.)

Samaritans –

(Look in telephone directory under 'S' for Samaritans.)

2. **Divorce and after**

Citizens' Advice Bureaux –

(Look in telephone directory under 'C'. Will give advice and direct inquirer to the appropriate agency.)

Legal Aid Department, The Law Society, 29 Red Lion Street, London, WC1 Telephone: 01–405–6991

Campaign for Justice in Divorce, Coombe House, Butler's Cross, Aylesbury, Bucks. Telephone: 0296–623687

Gingerbread, 35 Wellington Street, London, WC2 Telephone: 01–240–0953 (Self-help organisation for one-parent families, over 350 local groups and publications – i.e. housing, supplementary benefits and family law – also gives advice by letter or telephone. Penfriend scheme and Gingerbread Holidays – low-cost holidays for one-parent families.) National Advisory Centre on Careers for Women, 251 Brompton Road, London, SW3 2HB

The Open University, PO Box 48, Milton Keynes, MK7 6AB

3. **Money**

Department of Health and Social Security –

(Look in telephone directory under 'H' for Health.)

Child Poverty Action Group, 1 Macklin Street, London, WC2 5NH Telephone: 01–242–3225 or 242–9149 (charity working with, and on behalf of poor families, advice on

welfare rights and publications on poverty and welfare rights).
Citizens' Advice Bureaux
(Can advise and direct to correct agency.)
Bank manager
Professional accountant

4. Housing

Local Housing Department
(Look in telephone directory under name of appropriate borough or area.)
Housing Aid Centres
(Give help and information about housing. Ask at town hall or housing department, or Citizens' Advice Bureau.)
Local housing associations
(Look in yellow pages in telephone directory, under 'Housing'.) – for London and Greater London, contact:
The London Regional Office (of the Housing Corporation), Waverley House, 7–12 Noel Street, London, W1 Telephone: 01–434–2161
Citizens' Advice Bureaux
(Deal with lots of housing queries and can direct to appropriate agency.)
London Housing Aid Centre, 189a Old Brompton Road, London, SW5
(Advice on housing problems in London.)
Shelter, 157 Waterloo Road, London, SE1 8UU Telephone: 01–633–9377
(Publications and advice on housing problems.)
Catholic Housing Aid Society, 189a Old Brompton Road, London, SW5 Telephone: 01–373–4961
(Nationwide housing aid service – on a small scale.)
Church Army Housing Ltd., Welford House, 112a Shirland Road, London, W9 Telephone: 01–289–2241
National Women's Aid Federation, 374 Grays Inn Road, London, WC1 Telephone: 01–837–9316 or 837–3762 (will provide addresses of hostels for battered wives and their children).

5. Children

National Council for One Parent Families, 255 Kentish Town Road, London, NW5 2LX Telephone: 01–267–1361

(Assists lone parents by advice and publications, deals with inquiries by either telephone, letter or interview [appointment advised]. Makes positive proposals to Government, and helps and advises central and local authorities; gives legal advice.)

National Society for the Prevention of Cruelty to Children (NSPCC), 1 Riding House Street, London, W1 – 24-hour telephone service: 01–580–8812
(Local address in telephone directory under 'N' for National.)

Parents Anonymous, 49 Godstone Road, Purley, Surrey. Telephone: 01–668–4805
(Contact above for local addresses or telephone numbers. Self-help groups, telephone help lines, fact sheets about starting a group.)

The Salvation Army, Missing Persons Department, Middlesex Street, London, EC1 Telephone: 01–247–6831

Families Need Fathers, 10 Hartley Close, Bromley, Kent Telephone: 01–467–8319 (a society demanding a fairer system to deal with decisions about custody and access.)

Education Offices
(Look in telephone directory under 'E' for education – in the appropriate borough or area)

Other people who may be able to advise or help
local clergy
family doctor
welfare officer
probation officer
social worker
headteacher
health visitor

List of useful Books and Pamphlets

Alone Again, Angela Williams, NMGC, 1977.

Breaking Up, Rosemary Simon, Arrow Books Ltd., Hutchinson, 1974.

The Challenge of Second Marriage, Angela Reed, Plume Press/Ward Lock, 1975.

Death and Rebirth of a Marriage, A. & M. Havard, Scripture Union, 1969.

Divorce (the Biblical Teaching), John Stott, Falcon, 1971.

Divorce ... and After, Gerald Sanctuary and Constance Whitehead, Oyez Publishing, 1976.

Divorce and Your Money, Bill Hooper, George Allen & Unwin, 1979.

Guide for Home Owners, Jo Tunnard/Clare Whately, CPAG & Shelter, 1977.

The Half Parent, Brenda Maddox, Andre Deutsch, 1975.

Holiday Guide for One Parent Families, NCOPF.

How Christian is Divorce and Re-marriage?, Franklyn Dulley, Grove Books, 1974.

The Hurt and Healing of Divorce, Darlene Petri, David C. Cook Publishing Co., Ontario, 1976.

Marital Breakdown, Jack Dominian, Penguin, 1968.

Marriage and the Church's Task, CIO Publishing, 1978.

National Welfare Benefits Handbook, edited by Jo Tunnard and Nick Warren, available from Child Poverty Action Group.

One Parent Families ... Help with Housing, HMSO.

Second Marriage, Darlene McRoberts, Augsburg, 1978.

To have and to Hold, David Atkinson, Collins, 1979.

Also ... Leaflets about National Insurance, Income Tax, free school meals,
    FIS, Child benefit increase, etc., available from
    Department of Health and Social Security, Post Office and
    Citizens Advice Bureaux.

Leaflets about rent rebates, rates, heating, letting, legal aid, etc.,
available in libraries, council offices, Citizens Advice Bureaux.
NMGC Book Department, Little Church Street, Rugby, for list of recommended books and pamphlets for counsellors.